GW01045191

Captain Concorde

The True Story of One Man's Remarkable Journey of Flight and Faith

Brian Walpole OBE
with Graham Lacey

Grace & Down
Publishing

Dedication

In memory of my beloved wife Rosemary.

Throughout my journey,
the unfolding story of my life,
I delighted to have you by my side.
At peace now with our Lord in heaven,
I am assured I will join you there one day.

Thank you for everything, Brian x

Contents

Foreword by Josh McDowell

I've not read a book quite like *Captain Concorde* before – filled with the vast array of experiences of a man who excelled at all things flying, travelling at umpteen miles an hour, who then came to faith in a surprisingly pedestrian manner, with the help of a book I know well, as it was one of mine – *Evidence that Demands a Verdict*. Learning how my book helped Brian on his faith journey brought me immense joy as it is such an honour to play a small part in someone's journey to truth and understanding the reality of what Jesus did for each of us on the cross of Calvary. I truly believe *Captain Concorde* will capture the imagination of all, from the most cynical of engineers or scientists, to those who dreamt of flying on Concorde and never got the chance, to those who still have questions about salvation and who Jesus *really* is.

A delight to read, *Captain Concorde* is a wonderfully entertaining true story, sharing with the reader the unwavering excellence of a man clearly gifted for a purpose, who not only studied meticulously for his job, but also conducted an equally rigorous review of the Christian faith.

Thank you, Brian, for sharing your story with us, and allowing me to play a small part of that journey. May this book do all you hoped for and more.

Blessings,
Josh McDowell
Author and Apologist

PS: Did I mention Captain Walpole barrel rolled the Concorde?!

In recent times, I have not often written a foreword for a book whose author is older than I am. I mention this not to flag our respective ages, but to reference the near century-long experience of a man who wasn't "simply" a Concorde captain. Captain Walpole managed the whole of Concorde's operations to turn it into a vastly profitable part of British Airways history and, whilst doing so, welcomed royalty from all strands of society on board Concorde – be it the British Royal family, film stars, singing sensations or sporting greats from across the globe. Nonetheless, Brian eventually came to bow his knee to the ultimate in royalty, the *King of all Kings*, when he came to know the one person worthy of his unequivocal trust – Jesus Christ.

Acknowledgements

When you've passed your ninetieth birthday, there are invariably countless people who have impacted your life, many of whom are no longer still with us in this life, but they're nonetheless never far from our thoughts. My parents made many sacrifices for my brother and me and helped us navigate life in some hugely significant ways, some of which I touch upon in the pages which follow. My gratitude for all they did for us is immense . . . and has only increased as I became first a father, then a grandfather and latterly a great-grandfather. So, too, grew my wonder and awe at how my precious wife Rosemary gave life to all that our family stood for and the adventures we had together. My gratitude for all she meant to me knows no bounds and will remain until we meet again and for eternity in heaven.

Our three children mean the world to me, and I've delighted in seeing their own families grow and the burgeoning numbers as grandchildren and great-grandchildren are added to the fold. Shelley's deep faith has been a delight to behold, and her regular visits over the years from Vancouver have always brought great joy. Wonderfully Julie and Graham live much closer and I cannot thank them enough for the daily support and care (in ever increasing degrees) which they have shown me. My love for them all and immense pride in the people they are and in their individual and collective achievements is unbridled, and I hope these words remind them of that.

Professionally, in this book I acknowledge with immense gratitude the contribution of the entire Concorde team, the many highly skilled and committed people who I had the good fortune to train, fly and work with. At a more individual level, I have to start with acknowledging Jock Lowe. We shared the good times and challenges together. I am confident that had I not had his support and insights, and the benefits of his business brain, we would never have achieved the successes we came to enjoy at Concorde. His subsequent friendship was an added bonus. My gratitude equally goes to Lord King for believing in Concorde, and for giving me the opportunity to put the words from my many letters into actions; to George Blundell-Pound who was so instrumental in taking the Concorde experience to the wider public through the charter programme; and to Adrian Meredith for capturing so many of the iconic images of Concorde, a number of which adorn these pages, helping to ensure the legacy remains for generations to come.

Personally, there have been numerous individuals who have helped me over the years, some of whom have become like family, you have my respect and unfettered gratitude. Tracy, you have been a God-send to me. Adrian, your able hands have nurtured my garden for many decades, the beauty of which lifts my spirit daily. And, of course, my wonderful canine friend and 24/7 companion, Zephyr!

As you'll discover in the heart of this story, my journey of flight and faith was an interesting one, and I am indebted to the tennis commentator and journalist Gerald Williams for his unashamedly forthright approach; to Justin Dennison, who gave me such exceptional guidance; and to Bob Roxburgh, my first pastor, who later became my in-law! Jon Herring picked up the mantle at Gracechurch Leatherhead in later years, and his leadership and outreach continue to inspire myself and countless others. I have many dear friends there but to Mike Taylor and Ian Sneller especially – thank you for the enormous comfort, support, friendship and love we have shared over the years. And lastly to Josh McDowell, whose book *Evidence that Demands a Verdict* was such an integral part of my faith journey, as it has been for thousands across the globe.

My thanks regarding the creation of this book must go to Graham Lacey and TBN, for initially airing my story in the *Captain Concorde* documentary back in 2020, and to Ursula Ferguson, whose love of God, tennis and Concorde perfectly complemented the detailing of my journey on these pages. And finally, to my son Graham who first persuaded me of the value of sharing my story and, along with Ursula and the Mayflower team, has helped bring this book to life – it would not have happened without you, Graham, so on behalf of our entire family, Thank You!

Captain Brian Walpole OBE

Preface – Before We Begin . . .

"Here is the Bonham's lot number. I want this seat – it's important to me – so please make sure I get it, whatever the cost." My parting comment to my assistant, as I handed her the Concorde Charity Auction catalogue from British Airways and headed off to a meeting. It was an odd request, but she didn't argue; after all, this wasn't just any seat, it was a Concorde captain's seat, which had come up for auction and I, Graham Lacey, wanted it. At the time, such items being auctioned was a rare occurrence and not one I wanted to miss. Needless to say, the deed was done, and I became the proud owner of said captain's seat. But why the fascination with a Concorde seat? Simple really. I had crisscrossed the planet more than a hundred times on Concorde to buy and sell companies, meet with presidents and royalty, world and spiritual leaders alike, and the seat mattered to me, a collector's item, a memory of a time in my life, and the many fascinating people I met onboard the magnificent creation.

Flying at twice the speed of sound, Concorde's ability to transport me from London to New York in a little over three hours transformed my working life, as it did so many corporate leaders. As I wrote in my book *Take My Life*, I would use Concorde to attend a business meeting in NYC and then return for an important church meeting with R.T. Kendall in Westminster. We used to joke that I could leave London and arrive in New York for morning Board meetings "before I had even left". Flying faster than the speed of a rifle bullet, the captain could control Concorde with the fingertips of just one hand. One hand! But they were not just any ordinary hands. They belonged to the men and women who had all undergone rigorous training and, in one particular instance, to a man who not only barrel rolled the majestic aircraft, but also gave the late Queen Elizabeth II and Prince Philip a low-level Concorde flypast on the Royal Yacht *Britannia*. That man was Captain Brian Walpole OBE, and what follows within these pages, is his story of flight and faith.

Though I would fly frequently from LHR to JFK for a meeting, I never had the pleasure of sitting in one of the particularly unique seats on the flight deck. Housing four mounted seats in her cockpit, three of them belonged to the captain, first officer and flight engineer, and were all electronically operated with some of the most sophisticated technology used in civil aviation. The fourth, known as the jump seat, was wholly manual in operation and was set aside for a crew member should they need to sit there, though in reality it was more often filled with one of the many dignitaries who delighted in visiting the flight deck. Personally, I never made it to the heights of the jump seat, but flying Concorde was the norm for me. Little did I realise at the time, had it not been for Captain Brian Walpole, such trips may have been short lived. Although I have since had the pleasure to sit down and discuss this reality and his Concorde experiences at length, my rather inauspicious first meeting with Brian left me wishing I'd never opened my mouth. Embarrassed as I am to admit it, I had the audacity to criticise him whilst he was captaining a Concorde plane which had just been struck by lightning – not once, but twice!

We were on a flight to JFK, and Concorde had taken off from Heathrow and was flying past Windsor Castle when it was hit by lightning. A minute later, it was hit again. Whilst the plane's design means it is perfectly able to withstand a lightning strike or two, I now know that each time it is struck the crew have urgent matters to attend to. Requiring an immediate and urgent reboot of the computers for the plane to operate properly, having been struck twice, that procedure needed to happen twofold, in quick succession. It was at this most inopportune moment that a stewardess advised Captain Walpole that I, a frequent Concorde flyer, was outside the flight deck suggesting that a little more communication about *"what just happened"* would be welcomed by the passengers. With far more diplomatic language than I deserved, the captain's response was conveyed back via the filter of the stewardess. Explaining that he was currently rather busy trying to protect 109 lives and £50 million worth of equipment, it was suggested that perhaps now wasn't therefore the best time for my input. I, Graham Lacey, a man whose opinion President Nixon had sought, skulked back to my seat in shame, tail very firmly between my legs, a shadow of my former arrogant self. I had been firmly, and quite rightly, put in my place by the man known in the industry as *Captain Concorde*.

Forty years after our embarrassing "lightning" encounter, as I sat down in Captain Concorde's sitting room, I was once again reminded of my audacious behaviour in the midst of the mid-flight emergency. Little did I realise, when I so humbly returned to my seat having been rightly reprimanded by Captain Walpole, that many decades later, we would sit down to discuss not just his experiences flying Concorde but also our shared faith in God, as part of a documentary (also aptly titled *Captain Concorde*) for the Trinity Broadcast Network (TBN). Hugely grateful as I am to my long-time friends and TBN founders, the Crouch family, for giving us the opportunity to make the programme, it was an honour to once again be reunited with Brian and discuss the course his life had taken. To learn as I did of Brian's journey of faith discovery alongside his aviation adventures, and to meet his wife Rosemary, were delights in equal measure.

Reflecting on my own personal experiences of both Concorde and Brian, I have no hesitation in saying that Concorde truly was a magnificent aircraft, and Brian Owen Walpole OBE was quite simply a brilliant aviator who used his gifts to the max. His aviation prowess was recognised in 1983, shortly before his fiftieth birthday, when he was elected a Fellow of the Royal Aeronautical Society, and further still in 1985 when he was granted the Freedom of the City of London. Countless other honours and accolades were bestowed upon Brian over the many decades of his service, but perhaps none was more noteworthy than the OBE he received in the 1988 Queen's Birthday Honours list. No doubt amongst all the medals and awards, Brian also has Concorde memorabilia that would make many a Concorde fan weep with jealousy, not least the silver tankard he received from BA when he was awarded his OBE. Though he considers it his most prized Concorde memento, all the human accolades and acknowledgements still pale compared to the life-changing discovery Brian made when he explored the Christian faith. As he came to know Jesus, the central figure of Christianity, the implications of that discovery for both Brian, his family and indeed for all of us, set Brian on a path which would forever alter his destination.

Aside from our frequent travel on Concorde, my journey has been vastly different from Brian's, as I'm sure is the case for most. We do all nonetheless share one significant certainty in common, for there is a reality everyone will face. No matter where we were born, the colour of our skin, the money in our bank balance, the truth we've created for ourselves, whoever and wherever we are in the world, the Bible has a simple message for every single one of us: we each have a decision to make about the death of Jesus and its significance for our life. Jesus's death on the cross was the climax of His life and so too will be our own death: before we meet that moment, we each have a choice to make about our response to the death and resurrection of Jesus. For those not familiar with the life and death of Jesus, here is a summary acrostic to explain it briefly, using CONCORDE:

Consider this, the Bible teaches us about life after death, and heaven, the eternal home.

On the day of our death, if not before, we will each face God.

No-one who defies God (sins) and rejects Him, can enter heaven.

Christ Jesus died to take the punishment of our rebellion against God (sins) – we ALL do it.

On that day, what will you say when asked if you accepted that Jesus died for your sins?

Responding yes (repenting), will mean you are free from sin and welcomed into heaven.

Denying His gift of salvation means rejecting Jesus' invitation to be with Him; the alternative is hell.

Eternity is a long time, so choose wisely!

I know some people think that this is unfair and cruel of God, but my decades of faith and life with God have shown me He is far from unfair. God is the pinnacle of true justice, giving every human on the earth the chance to get to know Jesus and decide whether or not to accept the gift of salvation He offers each and every one of us. As Brian shares in his story, it is the most important decision each of us will ever make in our lives.

This journey with Brian has been a truly memorable experience, and a pleasure to undertake for all of us at

Mayflower. We pray it will encourage you, the reader, to either investigate God for yourself, or if already assured of your final destination, to share that hope with someone else.

Keep looking up!

Graham Lacey

1

The Captain's Prelude

As a Concorde captain, I quite literally had the best seat in the plane, looking out on the vast horizon as we flew towards 60,000 feet. Before me was 250,000 square miles of magnificent creation, which we traversed at Mach 2 (twice the speed of sound), meaning we were flying twenty-three miles every sixty seconds. Most of us cannot even begin to comprehend the reality of these staggering statistics. And as for the view – it's one which precious few have had the privilege to witness. In the captain's seat, just like the one Graham Lacey purchased from Bonhams, as you sped through the air you could see with the naked eye where the earth and space meet; the darker blue of outer space and the curvature of the earth gently existing in such close and electrifying proximity as depicted so stunningly in one of the iconic images produced by Adrian Meredith, the long-time photographer for BA.

Concorde's instantly recognisable adjustable droop nose, her streamlined body, delta shaped wings, expandable fuselage and most notable Rolls Royce Olympus turbojet engines with afterburners, were what enabled supersonic flight to occur. The product of fifteen years of design, planning, manufacture and testing, Concorde was quite simply an engineering masterpiece, and yet so much more beyond. Like flying a fighter jet, the engineering triumph that was Concorde, was very precise and exceedingly sensitive to handle. Throw-away comments that Concorde would expand during supersonic flight, gradually elongating an extra ten inches, never failed to wow! With the air passing over the hull at supersonic speeds, the metal heated up so much that it expanded, and the fact that all the carpets did not get wrecked every time was another remarkable design feature. To allow for such expansion, an engineering brainwave placed the interior of the plane on rails so that as the hull of the plane expanded (and contracted when returning to subsonic), the interior of the aircraft would not be impacted. Though ten inches is not much compared to Concorde's vast length, the impact of the expansion was not always fully comprehended, so on the occasion that a VIP was on the flight deck at the right time, I would often take my captain's hat and put it between two stanchions on the flight engineers instrument panel. As the fuselage expanded, the stanchions would move, thereby crushing the hat; proof, if it was needed, that I was not exaggerating!

Exhibiting hitherto unmatched wonders of innovation and ingenuity, Concorde heralded a new era, and single-handedly took air travel to new heights. Not surprisingly, Concorde was a source of great national pride and became the darling of the jet-setting elite. From rock stars and sporting heroes to supermodels, CEOs and royalty, they all flocked to sip champagne and dine on Concorde's caviar, to enjoy the unrivalled aura of thrill and luxury which she so exquisitely provided. Behind the scenes, life within the Concorde fleet was a seismic shift from the perceived public persona and her patrons were completely oblivious to the internal maelstrom of unrest orbiting the back-room corridors.

Concorde was the product of the tireless input of a multitude of brilliant minds, many of whom I knew well. From the initial designers, manufacturers and test pilots to the subsequent team of pilots, engineers, cabin crew, ground staff and others who managed her on a daily basis, Concorde required a village to make her work. It was through the invaluable contributions of this "Concorde family" spanning many decades, dating as far back as the 1950s when the idea of supersonic travel was first conceived, that Concorde was delivered into the hands of British Airways via the UK Government. Having undergone the first test flight in March 1969, Concorde made her first commercial flight on 21st January 1976. That same year, the British Government required British Airways to take ownership of seven Concordes and, with the fortune of good timing (which blessed so much of my flying career), I happened to be of the right age, seniority and experience as a Boeing 707 captain, to be invited on to the second conversion course for Concorde pilots.

I have often referred to Concorde as the beautiful bird, paralleling her flying capability and the aesthetic beauty of her double delta wings which were perfectly shaped for supersonic flight. I wasn't the only one – countless millions regularly looked up in awe at Concorde as she passed overhead. Equally, I was once quoted in a Sunday paper as saying that she was a demanding animal. Both were true. Behind the beautiful metal finish were some of the most complicated systems of civil aviation, and my first flight in command of her came in the summer 1976. The fulfilment of a long training programme, it was a thrilling experience knowing that I was responsible for this beautiful bird and the 109 lives she carried: 100 passengers and 9 crew. Concorde's Chief Test Pilot, Brian Trubshaw, described Concorde as "very slippery", which summed her up perfectly and was the reason we Concorde pilots tended to sit a little closer to the edge of our seats. Any less than textbook execution of critical manoeuvres, be they turns, climbs, descents or otherwise, and control of the aeroplane could slip away from us in seconds. The ease with which it was possible to over or under control her, is what kept the seat edge hot; after all, things can go wrong quite quickly when travelling at 1,350mph.

The life of a Concorde captain was exciting, tremendously demanding and hugely rewarding. Flying the aircraft, we were travelling faster than the rotation of the earth twelve miles below, and it was exhilarating. As we looked out on the celestial horizon it was awe-inspiring; an "other worldly" experience enjoyed by a rare few. Taking us to such great heights, Concorde was the ultimate in aeronautical engineering and her technical complexity and speed asked much of the pilots. Flying the subsonic 707 from London to New York, a flight time of a little over seven hours, would leave me physically fatigued.

The same journey in Concorde, whilst only half the time, equally left me physically exhausted but, unlike the 707, I was also mentally drained, such was the concentration required. It never ceased to weigh on me that, as with any airline captain, I had precious lives in my care, as well as the responsibility for a highly valuable plane, the most advanced civil aircraft in the sky.

That said, the rewards of flying Concorde were unmatched by any other earthly experience I've known. When you take off from London in the dark of the evening heading for New York and see the sun in the west, you know you're doing something slightly different because you're travelling faster than the sun is setting and are quite literally catching the sun. We were transforming civil aviation, pushing new boundaries and flying an aircraft which was universally admired. Within the industry, as Concorde pilots we were the envy of aviators from other airlines around the world, and never needed reminding just how fortunate we were. Concorde was an aeroplane which touched the lives of multitudes in so many different ways, not just the rich and famous. Many of those who lived on the Concorde flight path told me how the marvel of watching the beautiful bird overhead, an event which they could invariably set their clocks by, never diminished with time. Neither, might I add, did the honour of flying her.

Following many turbulent years behind the scenes, where the joy of flying supersonically was balanced with no shortage of technical, legal and operational challenges as we fought to achieve commercial success, I was invited to head up the British Airways Concorde division, and had the privilege of captaining Concorde on what would become some of her most historical "firsts". It was for this that I was flatteringly referred to by some as *Captain Concorde*. Of course, over the years there were numerous pilots of Concorde, 134 to be precise, and many of them have shared their stories and reflections in various books and memoirs, as I am doing now with my own very personal *raison d'être*. It's unequivocally true that Concorde redefined an entire era of travel and personally provided me with challenges, opportunities and experiences I could never have dreamt of, but it's not just my life with Concorde which motivated this manuscript.

As you journey through the book, you'll read stories and anecdotes from my life that the aviation world has blessed me with – some humorous, others tragic, insightful or otherwise – and I hope they might be of interest and justify the cover price you paid! While some may bring a smile to your face and others a tear to your eye, they are only part of the rich tapestry of my life into which something far greater, far more magnificent is woven. This book is also about that – sharing my life-defining journey of discovering who God is; the one true God I have come to know and to whom I owe everything in my life. It's that journey, alongside my sub and supersonic journeys, that I hope will intrigue, fascinate, and even motivate you to go on your own journey of discovery. If that happens for even one person, I will consider all the efforts for this book worth it, for they pale compared to the difference knowing God has made to my life. I only wish that discovery had occurred earlier on in my journey; a journey which began on New Year's Day 1934 when I, Brian Owen Walpole, was born into a world slowly but inexorably building up to war.

2

The Journey Begins

"We are now at war," my father said sombrely. It was September 1939, I was five years old and far too young to understand the words he'd spoken, but they still shocked me. My father had served with distinction in the Royal Navy during WWI, and had survived the sinking of two different ships which had been torpedoed, both times being rescued and returning immediately to service. He was my protector, the one who made bad things go away, ever positive, an optimist, a Christian, and survivor of WWI, so the severity with which he uttered these words left me in little doubt that this was a serious event. Today, as a father, grandfather and great-grandfather, I wonder how he felt when he uttered those words. How would he be able to take care of and protect his family? Did he understand what was to come? Was anyone ready for the journey ahead? I was too young to understand what was happening and couldn't appreciate it at the time, but in hindsight can see that the war and its aftermath of compulsory national service set me on the path to a life in aviation, to taking charge of the first commercial supersonic flight

to New York and the meeting of my ego with the God of the Christian faith.

War aside, my childhood was a very happy one, often spent playing alongside my brother with the family dog and cat, under the watchful eye of our loving and devoted mum and dad. Indeed, on reflection, I often wonder if the war time years brought with them a sense of adventure to a young boy in his youthful innocence, shielded from the fear that no doubt constantly pervaded the lives of my parents and every adult across the country. I remember the never-ending air raid sirens, the relief after the seemingly endless wait for the all-clear, the nights spent in the underground bunker at the bottom of our garden and the worry etched on my father's face as he emerged after a night of bombing to see if our family house was still standing.

I vividly recall our evacuation to a hotel in Southampton, my father on the platform waving us goodbye, his smile no doubt bravely masking his uncertainty as to when, indeed if, he would ever see us again; this was quickly shadowed by the endless bombing around our hotel that made my mother openly question whether we might actually have been safer staying at home with father. Following our eventual return home, my childish innocence saw me excitedly charging towards a downed Spitfire on the golf course to the rear of our garden. My mother, with towels in hand, approached more cautiously, while I jumped onto the wing and peered inquisitively into the cockpit. My youthful exuberance was quickly silenced, as I faced the sobering reality of a pool of blood in the bucket seat, the fallen aviator but one of nearly a million of the British

Armed Forces whose ultimate sacrifice delivered the freedoms in which the rest of my life has played out.

It was late 1940 when one evening my father drove a six-year-old me in his Morris over the beautiful Epsom Downs, home of the world-famous racecourse which hosts The Derby. He pointed to the red glow on the distant horizon some twenty miles away, and in a hushed voice sighed, *"My boy, that is London burning."* Unaware at the time, I was witnessing the Great London Fire Blitz that so nearly destroyed our capital city, the image of which to this day remains etched in my mind with a few other horrors I have since witnessed. Whether at school, at home, in the bunker or on the road, there was no escaping the war. As a child, it certainly was not a constantly terrifying burden for me, but there was still hardly a single day that it did not punctuate. Many a week at school involved the numbing news that a friend's parent had become a casualty of war, whether a serviceman lost in battle or a victim of the nightly raids. The emotions were always the same: a mix of terrible and incomprehensible sadness for my friend's loss; gratitude and relief at my good fortune that my parents were alive; and worry about if, or indeed when, that good fortune might run out.

As 1946 drew to a close, the war finally over, life returned to relative normality for me in my adolescent years. My younger brother Colin and I were sent to Epsom College, a British independent school set in acres of beautiful Surrey countryside. I have little doubt as to the enormity of the financial sacrifice faced by my parents to send us there, but can only hope they felt it was repaid in the way we both lived our lives, and I'm only sad that they did not live to see my Concorde years. I believe they would have enjoyed and felt pride in their son's achievements; they may even have been a little surprised! Though my structured mind favoured the sciences over the humanities, I was not known as an academic child. Nonetheless, having been encouraged to study hard by my parents, I soon found that if I knuckled down, I could actually make the grades and achieve something. My greater passion was always for the multitude of extracurricular activities on offer at school, not least the sport; I was probably never happier than when dressed in my white flannels on the cricket field, taking after my father who encouraged me greatly in this shared passion.

Whilst academically educated at Epsom, Colin and I were raised in a well-disciplined way at home, with what I suppose may be called good Christian values, but I would never claim that we were brought up in the Christian faith. Maybe this was because the deep belief of my father was not outwardly expressed by my mother. An avid nightly reader of his well-thumbed and gently fraying Bible, my father did not overtly incorporate his beliefs in daily family life. I recall once or twice attending church with him when I was young, but my brother and I were certainly not exposed at home to Christian teachings, nor were we taken to Sunday school every week. Far better is my memory of the odd occasions the pastor dropped into the house for coffee or a beer; I would sit on my father's knee enjoying listening to their conversation, even though I had no comprehension of what they were talking about!

Other than that, my experience of church was no more than an occasional outing for Christmas carols, weddings and funerals and held little significance for me. My father, however, was clearly a God-fearing man who took the Bible seriously and I have no doubt that he prayed for us and sought God's wisdom in the decisions he made for our family.

With the summer of 1951 came the conclusion of life at Epsom College, and the realisation that any plans I might have for the future would soon have to be paused whilst I fulfilled my two years of National Service requirements, a form of peacetime conscription which came into force in 1939 and remained in place until 1960. Not due to be called up until April 1952, I seized the opportunity to get six months of work experience under my belt at a stockbroker in the City of London. My time there ignited a passion for following the fortunes of companies on the stock market which has lasted throughout my life, and when my work experience was concluded, I left with a genuine conviction that stockbroking was where my future would unfold.

In the meantime, I had more immediate decisions to make. National Service required a commitment to one of the three armed forces: British Army, Royal Air Force (RAF) or Royal Navy. I knew my father had served with distinction in the Royal Navy in WWI, before joining the Home Guard in 1940 – set up as Britain's "last line of defence" against German invasion in WWII. I, however, had other ideas. I had relished my time in the Air Training Corps at Epsom College when I took full advantage of the opportunity to fly in a Dakota (military transport aircraft). An extracurricular activity like no other, it was adrenaline-charged, exhilarating and, most importantly, where I felt remarkably at home, quite possibly due to being gifted with good hand-eye coordination. Recognising that flying was where I felt most at ease, I determined the RAF was the route I would take and enrolled to get airborne. There followed a series of aptitude tests most notably around hand-eye co-ordination, involving endless hours of head scratching whilst staring at an array of square pegs and round holes. Bemusement aside, I must have made sufficient sense of them as I was duly accepted into the RAF, and unknowingly kick started what was to become the deeply fulfilling adventure of a lifetime.

Leaving the comforts and security of home, in 1952 my initiation into RAF life took the form of twelve hours of assessment in a Tiger Moth, a twin-seater single-engine biplane which would fly at 90mph and was probably the most famous training aircraft of all time. The initial phase involved more advanced aptitude tests which would separate the group into either aspiring *Pilots* or *Navigators*. Given the dashing public image of fighter pilots, it might surprise some that my own desire at the time was to be a navigator. The notion of sitting behind the pilot, making pen and paper mathematical calculations, mapping one's position by the stars, was captivating and appealed to my scientific mind. It was therefore with an initial tinge of disappointment that, while assembled in a hangar to hear the results of our aptitude tests, I was presented with the grades that determined my RAF trajectory was actually to be that of a pilot. The tests were there for a reason, and I trusted their process. Funnily enough, I know of a young man who at eighteen went forward for the aptitude tests to be a pilot. After the tests, which involved the requisite hand-eye coordination challenges as well as mathematical IQ assessments, he was called into a room and told, *"You're a mathematical genius, but we would not let you ride a bike!"* Thankfully, this damning indictment of his ability to fly was immediately followed up by an invitation to commence his navigator training, and he went on to become a hugely significant navigator for the RAF. Clearly their aptitude tests worked!

There was little time to dwell on my initial disappointment that I was not destined to be an RAF navigator; with our immediate futures sorted, we were straight back to training, in the open cockpits of the Tiger Moths. Throughout the course I remained under the watchful eye of an instructor seated no more than a few inches behind me. Whilst immensely thankful for his tutelage, I greatly respected and rather envied the small handful of my intake who proved themselves proficient enough to fly solo before the course was completed, a privilege and an experience I would have to wait a little longer to enjoy myself.

Those first months in the RAF were as much an initiation to the standards and disciplines demanded of us as young Acting Pilot Officers (APOs), as they were an initiation to flying. As in any military training institution, we were instructed on how to march, how to salute, the minimum boot shine requirements, the minimum buttoning up of our uniform when off duty, maximum hair lengths and countless other obligations concerning behaviour and appearance. I recall one time I was off duty when my contravention of these codes drew swift admonition from a passing military policeman. My unbuttoned uniform catching his gaze, he did not hesitate to stop me, point out that I was improperly dressed, insist I rectify the issue immediately and remind me in no uncertain terms of my APO dress code obligations.

Back on base, the enforcer in chief was the drill corporal, a seemingly rough brute of a man with few discernible redeeming features, who would walk up and down the line as we stood on parade every morning, pausing behind each of us as he inspected every fibre of our appearance. We could feel his breath on our necks as we awaited the barks of his vicious tongue and the humiliation which usually followed. On one such occasion, my own eyes fixed firmly ahead, the seemingly interminable silence as he lingered behind the recruit beside me was broken by the drill corporal's barked question, *"Am I hurting you?"* When the recruit dutifully responded, *"No, Corporal,"* he was met with the stern retort, *"Well I should be, I'm standing on your hair."* Tempting as it was to burst out laughing, I knew restraint was the wise option, and duly kept quiet, but it stuck with me. My son eagerly reminds me that it was a refrain I would later use often with my children when their hair was, to my stringent military standards, overdue a cut!

As a group of proud and excitable young cadets, countering the corporal's "humour" was inevitable, and it didn't take long for strategic alliances to form as we discussed a suitable response. Two of my fellow cadets were trained garage mechanics, one of them having been an employee of Austin, the British car manufacturer. These were skills and experience which came in very handy in our dalliances with the drill corporal, who just so happened to be the proud owner of a small Austin 7 motor vehicle. Parked every day in full view of the cadets, the Austin's location and our scheming minds were a tantalising combination and unleashed a delightful opportunity, which a group of cadets embraced with the customary zeal and enthusiasm befitting young military cadets' mischief.

The plan was to dismantle the Austin, part by part, and reassemble it on the top of the training block roof – what you might call, a vehicular relocation. Far too eager to put the plan into action, fuelled by fearless impudence, they were itching to get one over the corporal and didn't waste any time setting to work. The mechanical mastery of the garage mechanics in full flow, under cover of darkness, ladders duly positioned, the corporal's pride and joy was indeed dismantled into lumps and piece by piece of Austin 7 engineering was transported up the ladders and reassembled on the roof. The corporal's colourful language the next morning, whilst too ripe for these pages, gave testimony to the fact that the exercise proved to be well within the cadets' expertise and was a thunderous success. While individual involvement was never proved, the subsequent singling out by the humiliated corporal of certain cadets in the daily parade suggested that he had little doubt as to the identity of the perpetrators. To a man, the verbal bating they endured was considered a price worth paying, and I only wish today that I had photographic evidence of their exploits to share!

Cadet japery aside, once the Tiger Moth training was complete I graduated to its more powerful successor, the closed cockpit Chipmunk training plane, widely known as the "Chippy" and well feted for its aerobatic capabilities. The closed cockpit may have removed the air-in-the-face thrill of the Tiger Moth, but the contrasting ease of communication with the instructor was a welcome distinction. That said, I did not enjoy those comms with the instructor for long, as it was on the Chippy that I was to finally experience the first standout moment of any pilot's career – my maiden solo flight. A multitude of emotions were in play that day: the pride, the excitement, the sense of liberation of being totally alone, with maybe just a trickle of sweat betraying my slight adrenaline-filled apprehension. I loved it, and could not wait to tell my parents about it in the weekly call which had become part of our routine. Wherever I was posted, so long as I could find a phone box, I would always call them on a Sunday evening, and I took exceptional pride in sharing this experience with them that particular Sunday. It was life affirming, a moment I will always remember, and with their joyful enthusiasm for the milestone matching my own, I shared every memory with them as I recalled the overwhelming experience of my first unaccompanied flight.

With my first solo flight logged, I had ample opportunity to enjoy the experience of flying unaccompanied as the Chippy training required a further eight to nine hours of lone flying. Achieved with unfettered delight, I soon advanced to my next aircraft adventure for a year's course at Dalcross Airport in Inverness, which proved to be an equally unforgettable flying experience. After the Chippy came the Airspeed Oxford, or Ox Box as it was affectionately known. A highly manoeuvrable twin-piston engine propeller plane, the Ox Box had played a major role in the winning of WWII. Life at Dalcross exposed me to a multitude of exercises in the Ox Box, including flying with and without visual ground contact, relying on instruments alone when flying in cloud cover, and was yet another incredible adventure, not only from a flying perspective.

Away from the sky, my time at Dalcross heralded the start of my lifelong love affair with Scotland, a land whose rugged and dramatic beauty I have absorbed in wonder every one of the past sixty-plus years. Travelling to Inverness became a regular pursuit later in retired life, often to enjoy a round of golf at the stunningly beautiful Nairn Golf Club, which was a short drive along the coast of the Moray Firth. My many visits bore witness to the evolution of Dalcross Airport into today's Inverness International Airport, servicing what is now close to a million passengers a year. Seeing the old meteorology lecture hall which I'd spent many study hours in, and other buildings being retained and adapted, continued to evoke the deeply embedded treasured memories of that blissful early posting.

The good times at Dalcross were numerous, both in and out of the cockpit, a healthy social life revolving around the bar and weekly Saturday night outings to the local dance hall doing much to keep spirits high. Those good times, however, were agonizingly interrupted with sobering reminders that flying was not without its risks, even in peacetime. A number of my fellow young aviators sadly did not survive the year. One pilot I recall in particular, engaged and due to be married at the end of the year, had his life and dreams tragically cut short when he lost his bearings at night and flew straight into a hillside. Whilst we were never told the reason for the crash, we were painfully aware that his headstone could have carried any one of our names, and it was a chilling reminder of the risks we faced as young aviators.

The low-level, cross-country and night-time solo flying exercises culminated in me coming out top of my course and earning my wings. A meaningful moment in any pilot's career, my delight was once again shared by my parents, who took me to a celebratory lunch at the neighbouring Cuddington Golf Club when I was next home. I think they were becoming more assured that their son had a gift for flying and had made the right choice with the RAF, and so with the Dalcross course duly completed, it was time for the next phase of my fledgling flying career. The year was 1954, and a twenty-year-old me went south to Full Sutton outside York for what was to be the most technically demanding six-month conversion course I had thus far experienced in my training – little did I know what courses were yet to come in my career!

The course at Full Sutton involved conversion from a piston, such as the Ox Box, to a jet engine aircraft, which in my case was the Gloster Meteor 8, Britain's first operational jet fighter and the only Allied jet to see combat in WWII. Sent up in twin-seater versions of the jet for training by Fighter Command, I recall being struck by how vastly different they were; the required action and reaction times given the increase in speed from 150mph to 350-400mph, the handling, the instrumentation, the performance, and the greatly appreciated cockpit silence which was countered by much louder engine noise levels when outside the aircraft. It was a whole new experience and it was not lost on me that I had the fortune of doing something which very few twenty-year-olds had the opportunity to do – flying in a jet at ever increasing speeds. Suitably hooked, I immersed myself in every aspect of the comprehensive course as we became familiarised with the huge upgrade in performance of jet flying. My fascination with jets motivated me to achieve more top grades, which were to serve me well as a newly signed up squadron member.

With the conversion course to jets successfully completed, it wasn't long before I was posted to a fighter squadron with an operational unit teaching us air-to-air firing. Training over the sea off the beautiful Northumberland coast, trainees were required to fire at a banner trailing behind another Gloster Meteor plane, the accuracy of each pilot's shot evidenced by the different colours of bullets displayed (or not, in some cases) on the banner when it was brought down to land. After firing our rounds, we would push the plane to its limits of around 300mph as we returned to the airfield, before slowing and turning to land. One morning, congregating after our own individual sorties to observe our fellow pilots from the comfort of an anteroom, our chat was brought to an abrupt and shocking end as we witnessed an out-of-control Gloster flying low, at maximum velocity, directly over us.

The plane lost height some distance from the airfield and disintegrated on ground impact into a ball of fire. Subsequent investigations revealed that a solitary bird had smashed through the front cockpit window and killed our fellow pilot. Witnessed by us all, this was yet another uncensored warning of the unavoidable dangers we encountered every time we took to the skies. As young men a little more mindful of our future hopes and aspirations, it also provoked a more empathic recognition of how much greater the risks, pain and suffering must have been just a decade earlier for the young men in the prime of their lives, who had been faced with the ravages of wartime combat during WWII. At the time we were too young to fully comprehend the agonies of war, but now as we mourned the loss of our fellow cadet, the reality was tangible and the heartbreak genuine. Knowing the arbitrary flight of that bird could so easily have been directed into one of our planes, was a sobering experience for each one of us, and as we continued in service to our country, the potential for a brutal end to a life journey was never far from our conscience.

3

Choosing a Flight

My National Service flew by, quite literally and also figuratively, and I was soon faced with another career decision – leave the Air Force or extend for at least two more years. Those considering staying were offered a £500 incentive to do so, but for me, it wasn't about the money, although it would be a very welcome addition to my "car upgrade" fund. The way I saw it, I'd done the hard work – the intensive training, the hours of studying, early mornings and drill corporals barking at me – and it would be a shame, a waste even, if that was all brought to a grinding halt. Leaving now would seem to render it all redundant and for nothing, and that did not sit well with me. So, with great enthusiasm, decision made, I signed on for another two years. With the extra £500 in my account, I continued on to Horsham St Faith in Norwich flying Meteors with 74 Squadron – Tiger Squadron, as it was better known – one of the most prestigious in the history of the Royal Air Force. Tiger Squadron's rich history, with key roles in the Normandy invasions and the Battle of

Britain, before ending the war operating from bases inside Germany, give credence to the squadron's reputation.

Not surprisingly, the squadron attracted some of the most experienced fighter pilots in the RAF ranks. When I arrived, many of my fellow airmen had recently returned from the Korean War, and several were proudly adorned with their Distinguished Flying Crosses. Needless to say, it was daunting company for a highly impressionable, newly qualified pilot to join, but I loved it, finding every facet of squadron life exceptionally enjoyable and deeply rewarding; from the finesse of operational flying in the Gloster Meteor 8, an aircraft I grew to love, to the tremendous bonhomie amongst the pilots, of all ranks and experience. I appreciated my time there and learned so much from all aspects of life in Tiger Squadron.

At the time, chaplains were commonplace in the RAF. Having been introduced to the British Forces for religious instruction in 1918, the chaplains provided much support to troops during the traumas of WWII. Though I participated in remembrance parades and carol services, I'd not taken much notice of the chaplains; their offer of a chat or prayer was never something I felt I needed, preferring as I did to seek wisdom either from my father, or more frequently to resolve my own questions and submit to the fate I believed I could orchestrate by my own efforts and achievements. Such indifference to the chaplaincy, however, began to soften during my time at Tiger Squadron, where I progressed from Pilot Officer to Flying Officer, and had more interactions with the chaplain assigned to our squadron.

The chaplain was a charismatic man whose manner fascinated me, often appearing in the recreation room where we were relaxing and having a coffee after a flight. Whether enquiring about how the flight had gone or sharing something from his faith, I warmed to him. He did not preach at me, but rather spoke candidly and with conviction about the reasons he had for his active faith, and I was interested in how he shared his beliefs. Our conversations became more regular and I came to know him not just as the chaplain, but as one of the men, and over time we actually became good friends. Such was the extent of our friendship that years later he even featured in my wedding day.

It was during one of our early interactions, sharing his faith as he did, that the chaplain gave me a little book called John's Gospel. Smaller than my hand in size, it was an extract from the New Testament of the Bible, and the first edition had on the front cover:

THE GOSPEL ACCORDING TO ST JOHN
"ACTIVE SERVICE"
1914-18
PLEASE CARRY THIS
IN YOUR
POCKET
AND
READ IT EVERY DAY

Designed specifically for troops during WWI, the book was small enough to fit in one's pocket, which given the encouragement to read it was an important design feature.

Noteworthy also, in the version updated for WWII which I received, was the message inside from King George VI:

"To all serving in my Forces by sea or land, or in the air, and indeed, to all my people engaged in the defence of the Realm. I commend the reading of this book. For centuries the Bible has been a wholesome and strengthening influence in our national life, and it behoves us in these momentous days to turn with renewed faith to this Divine source of comfort and inspiration."

September 15, 1939

Alongside the words from John's Gospel in the Bible, with underlining of certain key verses throughout to make reading it simple for the troops, the book also included two wonderful hymns. "Rock of Ages" and "Abide with Me" were known to service men and women up and down the country, and though we might not have realised it at the time, each rendition served as a prayer to the God of the Christian faith, for help and protection. The little booklet, no more than five millimetres in depth, closed with a word from the Naval & Military Bible Society, who produced it:

What the compass and instruments are to the naval officer and the ordnance map is to the field officer, so the Bible is to us in our **journey through life**.

This Gospel will give you guidance and help for each day.

When you have read it through, you will find still greater help in the complete New Testament (Service Edition) obtainable from: Naval & Military Bible Society, Eccleston Hall, London, SW1.

Though I gave it a superficial read, it didn't mean that much to me in terms of the deeper meaning, but I would come to understand that the Bible's relevance to our *journey through life* is infinite. Appreciating as I do now the words of the Bible Society, at the time I certainly did not consider its value to my life journey equivalent to the value I bestowed on a compass as I navigated the skies. Thankfully, when the chaplain gave me the Gospel, he summarised the message for me; that it told the story of Jesus, who came to earth to save all humanity. Though I did not really understand what that meant and had no idea what we all needed saving from, something about what the chaplain said stuck with me, as did the little book. One of the most impacting parts of his message for me, came in his authenticity and delivery – it was evident that the chaplain was not just doing his job, but actually believed the message from the Bible which he was sharing and I surmised that just as my father had done so, the chaplain clearly took what the Bible said seriously.

With the chaplain's words flying around in my thoughts, whilst I did not read it every day, I did do as the old cover suggested and placed the Gospel in the chest pocket of my flying suit, purposely next to my heart. In simple terms, I felt this would keep me safe! With me on every flight, my rationale was that if I had it with me, the God of that Gospel would save me if I got into difficulty. Had I actually taken the time to read it, I might have been more reassured, but carrying it with me was all I managed at the time. Though my approach was flawed in terms of logic or sound reasoning, the chaplain's words and gift of the Gospel had clearly made an impression and reacquainted me with its main subject, Jesus. Like most people of my generation, I knew the story of Jesus through scripture lessons at school. I was also quite familiar with the circumstances surrounding his birth due to Christmas carol singing, which I had enjoyed doing on a number of occasions with a friend called Rosemary Blake, and others from the local villages when we were young children. However, my awareness of who Jesus is, and what that means for us in the twenty-first century, had been heightened by the chaplain's gift and had now entered my radar as never before.

Wider society has a saying that "timing is everything", often quoting it to explain surprising instances and events, either good or unpleasant. There are also many verses in the Bible about time, such as *"There is a time for everything, and a season for every activity under the heavens"* from the book of Ecclesiastes 3:1, or in the book of Romans 5:6 where it says, *"You see, at just the right time, when we were still powerless, Christ died for the ungodly."* Evidently from these verses, though I was not aware of it, time has a purpose and significance in God's plans as well. Whether you approach time from society's perspective or from the Bible's, my life's experiences most certainly point to the significance of timing, this being never more evident in my young life than in the extraordinary opportunity afforded me while in Tiger Squadron.

The year was 1955, I was twenty-one years old and the hierarchy of RAF Fighter Command had decided that it wanted to have a representative formation aerobatic flying team, with a view to promoting the Royal Air Force as one of the national services. As a result, all twenty-plus fighter squadrons across the country were invited to assemble their own four-man formation aerobatic teams, from which one would be chosen to represent the RAF. This team would be the forerunner to the Black Arrows and then subsequently the Red Arrows as we know them today.

Formation aerobatic flying should not be confused with the less complex formation flying, which displays aircraft flying in a straight and level pre-determined formation, such as the many fly pasts we've seen go over Buckingham Palace for different notable occasions. Formation aerobatic flying, however, is another level, very much based on exhibition flying, to show the skill of the pilots and the flexibility of the aircraft, both of which would be necessary to out-manoeuvre enemy aircraft. Demonstrating the precision and the level of control of the aircraft by the pilots, four aeroplanes in various combinations would perform rolls, loops and other carefully chosen manoeuvres. Always meticulously coordinated as they stayed together as a four in whatever shape was deemed appropriate for the occasion, the wing tips were just a few feet away from each other. Selection for such a team was understandably based on ability – who could handle his aeroplane sufficiently well and safely to get involved in the exhibitions of loops and rolls. Requiring exceptional skill, selection was a considerable notch on one's RAF belt. To add to the competitive edge at Tiger Squadron, the commander himself was part of the four, which made his selection process even more rigorous, as his life would be in the hands of the other three pilots given the proximity of the wing tips.

At the time it was policy at Tiger Squadron to assess the flying performance of its members every six months. Costs of training were substantial, and those not making the grade would need to be relocated. As part of the assessment, members would fly straight and level in formation (not aerobatic), practising on the wing tips of the other planes, whilst another plane conducted air-to-air firing. It wasn't long before the Squadron Commander called me to his office for my first assessment. As I stood before him, a surreptitious glance at my file lying open on his desk gave me a welcome boost; the word *"exceptional"* clearly decipherable in his rugged handwriting at the top of the page. An instant encouragement as I stood to attention, that the Commander saw such promise in me so early in my time at Tiger Squadron was hugely reassuring. Given his judgement on my flying competency, it was maybe not a great surprise that I was selected to join Commander Johnson's four-man team, but that made it no less thrilling. An honour for each of the four men to represent the squadron, for me even more so since I was the most junior pilot of the four and would be flying alongside some of the country's most experienced aviators.

Having achieved the personal honour of representing Tiger Squadron, the next challenge was for our squadron to win the right to represent the RAF as its official aerobatics display team. The selection process required each squadron to give a demonstration of formation flying to senior officers of Fighter Command and when all the squadrons had completed their submission, to our huge delight, Tiger Squadron came out on top and were awarded the collective honour. One of the most extreme difficulties in formation aerobatic flying is changing from one shape to another. For example, from line abreast to line fore and aft: the repositioning of the aircraft required in order to produce the next shape formation. Swapping these positions was by far the most complex and dangerous aspect of formation aerobatic flying, since it all happens within such close proximity of wing tips.

Given the nature of our working relationship, in between flights the four of us often sat in the recreation room together, discussing different formations we might try or reflecting on close calls of previous formations. It is safe to say that flying in formation at 350mph with your wing tips four feet apart was an adrenalin-fuelled experience which swiftly forged some trusted bonds between us, but it did not leave an awful lot of room for error. Thankfully, only once (in practice) did we get it a little wrong, resulting in the tail of my aeroplane being touched by a fellow aircraft. During a formation change, you have to move in various different directions, slowing down a little, moving a little closer or further out from the other aeroplanes, and it was during one such manoeuvre that the tail of my aircraft was touched by the nose of another.

Our squadron commander was the lead aeroplane and I was second on the right-hand side of his position, with the third to his left and fourth to the aft (behind us all). As the fourth aeroplane came into formation, its nose made contact with the tail of my aircraft and we all immediately broke formation. My instant concern was whether the come together had affected the control on my rudder, which would mean I would have no control for landing. As memories from training came flooding back of all those practised ejections we did on the ground from the ejector platform, shooting up to about thirty feet to experience the feeling, I wondered if this was to be the time where I experienced the real thing, or did I still have an aeroplane I could land? Thankfully, I soon deduced that the bump mercifully did not interfere with any of the controls, and suffice to say I was especially happy to land the aircraft in one piece that day. Once back on terra firma, our inspection showed nothing more severe than a few dents. Whilst I had experienced a number of close encounters, especially when practising our formations in the RAF, this was by far the closest I had come to pulling the ejection handle.

Flying regularly as a side activity in the RAF aerobatic team at air shows across Europe was an electrifying experience for a young man in his early twenties. However, as I had experienced at Dalcross, the dangers of life in the air were never far away and would arbitrarily reveal themselves, keeping our youthful sense of invincibility firmly in check.

The most brutal such instance I recall was during an air display in Manchester. Flying before us was the "Wing Man", a parachutist we had observed on numerous occasions previously at air shows, with bird-like wings strapped to his body, who would jump from a Dakota. We would be in the air, holding our formation as he did so, ready to follow his performance with our own, and so had the perfect bird's-eye view to witness his show at multiple events.

Tragically, on one occasion we were too close for comfort as we watched the Wing Man exit the plane. Instead of his usual display, he fell like a stone to his tragic death. This hardly put us in the frame of mind to perform our display but we were nevertheless ordered to proceed, with the aim of distracting the crowds from the terrible tragedy. The horror of witnessing his death has remained with me to this day, possibly even more so because of what we later discovered. The investigation evidenced that the Wing Man's fingertips were raw from his frantic efforts to activate his parachute pull cord (the rope which pulls the parachute out of its bag into the air). Chillingly, it was also reported that the night before the show, the Wing Man had dreamt of the impending disaster and the following morning had implored his superiors to cancel his show. Regrettably for him and his loved ones, the Wing Man's forewarning was ignored and he was instructed to do his job, discounting his foreboding dream and fears, and sending him to his tragic death. The timing of his dream and subsequent death has stayed with me –

a heart-breaking life lesson to heed those nudges or inner promptings regardless of other, often louder voices.

The tragic events during my stint with Tiger Squadron were conversely intertwined with many life-affirming and inspiring memories, and with time in all senses flying by, further decisions were on the horizon. I was coming up to four years in the Air Force, and whilst still with Tiger Squadron, the commanding officer informed me that the RAF were offering me a permanent commission. Though a job for life, the commission brought with it the likelihood that my time in the air would be severely curtailed. Post-war demand for Fighter Command pilots was understandably lessening, so staying in the Air Force would mean surrendering the rest of my life to their post-war priorities, which would increasingly be executed from the ground and not the air.

In the aviation world, we have the expression of "flying a desk", which means a qualified pilot working in a desk job. Given my passion for flying, this prospect posed a significantly unappealing downside to accepting the RAF commission. Another obvious alternative was to move into civil aviation – the formative thought being that civil aviation meant flying for life. Even more extreme, I could leave flying altogether and head to the City of London to rekindle my love affair with stockbroking, which had been so abruptly halted by my National Service what seemed a lifetime ago. Though still holding a candle for that short-lived corporate experience, I would still be seated at a desk and not in a cockpit, which diminished its appeal as a long-term prospect. I believed I had been given an ability to fly, and I wanted to make the most of the opportunities I had been given, and not waste them.

Before making my decision, I turned as I often did to my father for the benefit of his wisdom, and his advice was simple and favourably straightforward. If I really wanted to be in the sky and fly high, as he knew I did, then my best option was civil aviation. Stockbroking was not even a discussion. His rationale made sense, resonating with those inner promptings I was now more conscious of. Having helped with every big call in my life up to that point, my father's advice was good enough for me, and the decision was made. I was to leave the RAF where I had enjoyed a few incredible, life-defining years, and find a new home flying commercially in the world of civil aviation.

4

Welcome Aboard

Leaving the familiar confines of RAF accommodation, I returned home to my parents to begin studying for another conversion course – the Civil Aviation Authority (CAA) exams. Life at home was a far cry from the RAF years, but preparing for the world of civil aviation was not the only culture change I experienced in the late '50s. It was during this time that I also started the adventure of a lifetime, which would kick start many decades of married life with one of my carol-singing friends. Both living in Ewell, a small village in Surrey, Rosemary and I met when I was seven and she was just three – a meet cute of sorts. Our parents were friends and so time together became a regular occurrence. Living a mile up the road from us, Rosemary's family had a little swimming pool at their house, which proved to be a very popular place for my brother and me to spend time with Rosemary and her sister Jean.

Studying hard for my CAA pilot's licence at home, I will never forget the day my mother came upstairs and proposed I take a break, a suggestion which was to impact the course of my entire future. In true maternal style, Mother proceeded to inform me that she had just seen young Rosemary Blake walk past with her dog and suggested I ring her up and take her out. I recall thinking at the time that anything would be better than another full day of rather dry paperwork, so I made the call and offered to take her out for tea near Box Hill – a twenty-minute drive which would allow ample time for me to impress her with my much-adored car. Received with delightful positivity, my invitation was accepted and I drove round the next afternoon in my beautiful Austin Healey. She was my motoring pride and joy, so it was a rather inauspicious start to our date when Rosemary mistook it for the Triumph TR2 sports car! I tried not to be too offended, which was made all the more achievable by how delightful Rosemary's company proved to be. Though some might consider it cliché, I don't mind admitting, for me at least, it was love at first sight. What started as a cup of tea to distract me from my CAA exams, proved to be the *second* most important decision of my life; though at the time, I obviously considered it the *first*!

In June 1956 aged just twenty-two, with my little John's Gospel safely transferred from my flight suit to my new briefcase, having successfully passed the CAA exams I joined British Overseas Airways Corporation (BOAC) and officially entered the world of civil aviation. BOAC was the British state-owned airline, which was later to become British Airways, as it still is today. Thankfully for me, civil aviation was expanding at the time, with fully trained pilots from the military understandably of great appeal to the airlines. This fact wasn't lost on me when I interviewed with BOAC and received a very warm welcome, owing to my RAF record, which (editor adds) was exemplary. Joining as a junior co-pilot, it was a humbling experience; I had come from the RAF where I had been flying fighter jets and had been in the formation aerobatic team, top of the stack dare I say it. But then, on arrival at BOAC I was the most junior of the junior pilots; not only that, instead of flying at 600mph, we were now only flying at 180mph, so the whole thing took a bit of swallowing as I realised I was once again a nobody! It was another full year of yet more training before I was accepted to fly the BOAC Argonaut aircraft, which I would go on to pilot until it ceased operations a few years later.

With the sixties rolling in, the changes in my life were coming thick and fast. I had been out with other ladies, but Rosemary was the first meaningful relationship I had been in, and less than three years after our first date, on 31st January 1959 at a church in Ashtead, Ms Rosemary Blake became Mrs Brian Walpole, with my chaplain friend from Tiger Squadron performing the ceremony! Though we had to delay it due to work commitments, when we eventually got to go, we enjoyed a wonderful honeymoon in Malindi, on the Indian Ocean coast of Kenya. Today, a bustling metropolis and home to many luxurious hotels, but at the time Malindi was a traditional fishing village, with beautiful white tropical beaches, clear waters and a warm climate: perfect for a young married couple and the opening chapter of our shared love of Africa.

Newlywed with jets clearly the future of civil aviation, and the Boeing 707 leading the way, I was sent on yet another, thankfully successful, conversion course. The 707 was a magnificent aircraft, and it took me all over the world at what was a highly rewarding time to be flying; the only downside being the long absences from my new bride. That said, I didn't need to worry about Rosemary, who was very involved in the local community and had some wonderful friendship groups. One such was her music group, who met regularly for informal sessions, with Rosemary on the piano, a violinist and others participating as well. The local community enjoyed their various amateur concerts of classical music, with Chopin a regular favourite featuring in their repertoire. The group proved a delightful way for Rosemary to enjoy her love of music, which remained very much part of our lives together.

Flying commercially was new, exciting and rather extravagant; a time when passengers dressed up to travel; when meals were served with silverware and bone china; when leg room was expansive and interior designs luxurious. It was the "Golden Age" of air travel, before package holidays, wide-bodied planes and low-cost airlines heralded a more commoditised flight experience. Less golden were the smoke-filled cabins and flight decks, as cigarettes, cigars and even pipes were all permitted, their odorous waste lingering long in the pressurised cabins. When the eventual changes made by BA in that regard finally arrived, they were welcomed with open arms and healthier lungs by crew and passengers in equal measure.

In those early BOAC years, many of the captains I flew under as a junior co-pilot were vastly experienced former WWII bomber pilots. Given the average age of a WWII bomber crew was under twenty-five, some as young as sixteen, and the survival rate was little more than fifty per cent, it's somewhat surprising that they rarely credited their survival to good fortune and most certainly never "thanks to God". Invariably larger-than-life characters, operating in their own eccentric and autocratic styles, they were seldom ones to invite or accept challenges to their decision making, relying staunchly on their own abilities and judgement. No doubt, at that time in my life I too was leaning on my own wisdom, and would not have hesitated to attribute my success and survival exclusively to my own skill and heroics.

In hindsight, it saddens me that God seldom came into the equation and was not discussed more during those years of my life. That said, I wonder if the wisdom I often sought from my father was actually rooted in the wisdom he gained from his voracious study of God's words and teaching in the Bible. Maybe I actually had more appetite for biblical wisdom back then than I realised, being drawn to it as I was in others, such as with my father and the chaplain?! Or was it the opposite? Was God in effect pursuing me? Suffice to say, at that time in my life I did not give either of these possibilities a second thought, as I was far too focused on my flying. Nonetheless, I had my little John's Gospel tucked in my briefcase and regularly repeated what had become my flight prayer ritual of, *"God, please help me today."*

To my great delight, piloting and navigating were intertwined in that period of my flying career. At the time a 707-crew consisted of the captain, the flight engineer, and two co-pilots – one of whom would navigate on the outward journey, with the second navigating the return. It was therefore a requirement for a fully qualified co-pilot to also possess a navigator's licence, which qualified you to navigate a 707 anywhere in the world. Achieved through another taxing year-long course, which I'm sure wasn't much fun at home for Rosemary, once qualified, one of the most gratifying achievements for me or any BOAC co-pilot was to successfully navigate from Tokyo to Honolulu. This was an eight-hour flight during which the middle five to six hours were navigated solely by astronavigation, or celestial navigation as it's also known; a process whereby navigators determine the position of the aircraft relative to stars or other celestial objects.

During those middle hours the navigator was required to conduct a complicated series of calculations using a sextant (like a periscope) up through the roof of the aircraft to identify the optimum star to fix upon. Once a star had been pinpointed, the navigator would look up the star in the massive volumes of star data books we had on board. After identification, the navigator would then "shoot the stars", a navigation term for looking at the star through the scope for thirty seconds to a minute, to enable the position of the plane to be plotted. Taking the reading of the position of the star off the sextant, the process would be repeated again with two other stars. Once completed, the navigator would then have the requisite data to make calculations based on the position of the three stars; the location of the stars creating a triangle from which the position of the aircraft could be plotted. Comparing this with the anticipated position, you would hopefully find that you were on the right path!

Personally, I found plotting the location using the stars very gratifying. Often you would plot the positions and end up with lines between the three positions creating a triangle, with space in the middle (which could be quite a large area) – meaning somewhere in that triangle was your location, and your accuracy was wanting! Even more gratifying was when you chose three stars and plotted them on a chart and they all intersected perfectly, giving you your exact position. One distinctive drawback to this form of navigation, however, was that when cloudy, you lost visibility of the stars, and therefore would have to fly on a predetermined approximate heading until you managed to get a position from the stars, as without being able to see them, you are not able to "shoot the stars". Certainly, on occasions, we plotted our course only to fly into cloud and were forced to continue using navigation by estimation; the pre-determined heading was followed, and we then verified our position by star shooting once we had exited the cloud cover.

Shooting the stars was a complex and demanding procedure. From the moment the aircraft was out of range of the locator beacon at the departing airport, to the time the pilot advised we had the beacon of our destination airport coming up on our dials, the navigator worked relentlessly with these calculations. Having selected the three stars by which one intended to navigate, the course of the flight was in the navigator's hands. After 4,000 miles of flight, at an extreme the plane could be as much as fifty to a hundred miles off course, so locating the first beacon on approach always served as a welcome confirmation that your calculations were accurate, and was regularly followed by a muffled, *"Phew, we found it,"* from the navigator.

The simple reality was that in those days, long before the advent of GPS, there was no other way to navigate that "over-the-sea" route without using the stars, and it was a notable feather in one's cap when successfully completed. Having the opportunity of navigating once again was a thrill for me, reminding me why that pang of regret had arisen in my early RAF days, when told I would be a pilot not a navigator. I hasten to add, it did not last long and I have never regretted the path my life took as a pilot. Nonetheless, the mental challenge of navigation was a much-venerated puzzle to solve, and I was immensely proud when my navigator's licence was achieved.

Inevitably, navigators were under the most intense pressure during long flights, requiring great powers of concentration with curtains drawn around them as they carried out their intricate calculations. With the captain front left, co-pilot front right, navigator behind the captain and flight engineer behind the co-pilot, the flight deck was cramped and didn't always provide the most conducive environment for navigators who understandably, given the need for intense focus, did not appreciate disturbances. Never did I experience this truth more perfectly exhibited than the time I was a co-pilot and the junior navigator, faced with the challenge of the captain having nonchalantly placed his coffee mug on their navigational charts, elected to instruct a sudden change of course in order to, as he bravely put it, *"navigate around your coffee cup, Sir"*. His sense of humour was not appreciated by the captain, but point well made, and cup removed, no detour was necessary and we continued on the original course.

As in my RAF years, the pressures shouldered by flight crews often found their release valve in humour. As pilots, we generally got on very well with the cabin crew; we were on the same team and had tremendous respect for their professionalism and the calmness they exhibited in what were often highly stressful situations. Needless to say, that respect did not act as a barrier to us playing pranks on each other, often with the newest recruits being the best targets. On one occasion, on a flight from Benghazi, Libya, to Kano, Nigeria, a new stewardess upon seeing its extension through the roof of the fuselage, showed a particular interest in the navigator's use of the sextant. We suggested that when she came back to the flight deck she might enjoy the opportunity to look through it. Excited by the offer, she enthusiastically reappeared, pressed her eye tight to the cup and gazed in audible wonder at the stars. With an obvious skip in her step, she headed back to the cabin, only to be greeted by puzzled looks from the passengers. Concluding that something was awry, she dashed to the loo, where a look in the mirror revealed a jet-black ring circling her right eye, the result of our application of black boot polish to the eye cup of the sextant. It was rather mean, I know, but the camaraderie was strong, and we all had our moments and laughed about them afterwards, but perhaps not as heartily as we did over another incident involving a meal which was brought to the flight deck.

Much has been said about aeroplane food over the decades, but one occasion has forever been imprinted at the forefront of my mind when the topic is mentioned. In this particular instance another stewardess fell foul of the rather unconventional sense of humour of the captain we were flying with. As his co-pilot, my instructions were simply to aid and abet, a strictly non-speaking role, I was informed. As a common procedural safety requirement at the time, and I believe still with some airlines today, each member of the flight crew ate a different meal in case of food poisoning or other food-related problems. On this occasion, as the stewardess delivered our different meals, the captain requested sick bags from her for any food waste, to keep his flight deck clean and clear. The bags were thus delivered, and once the stewardess had left the flight deck the captain told me to pour my untouched meal into the bag. Recalling my *aid and abet* instructions, I did as I was asked, after which the stewardess was swiftly summoned back to the flight deck to be advised that use of the bag had proved necessary, given my violent, adverse reaction to the meal I had received.

Whilst it was no Oscar winning performance, my bent over, moaning demeanour and the expanded sick bag clearly convinced her that there was an issue, and she immediately offered to dispose of the bag. Much to her obvious surprise, the captain declined the offer, with the bold statement, *"No, we waste nothing on my flight deck,"* echoing loud for us all to hear, so we were in no doubt of his intentions. Her surprise rapidly turned to utter horror as the captain summarily grabbed the bag, opened it and proceeded to swallow its entire contents with great relish and much licking of lips. Eye wateringly disgusting, his flawless execution of the wind-up only served to exacerbate the ruse, triggering gag reflexes for those not privy to the more wholesome reality of what he had just consumed. With light-hearted pranks proving an outlet and part and parcel of crew life, the stewardess saw the funny side, along with the rest of the cabin crew, who had no doubt given her a heads up when she joined the team that some such shenanigans would likely occur.

Flying 707s was overall an exceptional job. Regularly rostered on ten-day round the world trips, I was exposed to a richness and diversity of countries and cultures, alongside the simultaneous painful demands of operating across multiple time zones and the sleep deprivation which this induced, whilst being away from Rosemary and our now blossoming young family. Amongst other considerations, it was recognition of these demands on flight crews by BOAC management that led to the emergence of overseas postings for certain crew. Highly popular among the crews, for me this resulted in a posting to Hong Kong in 1964 to fly the Asia Pacific routes, providing the onward travel link up to Tokyo and down to destinations like Australia and Honolulu for the flights arriving from London.

Based at the beautiful Repulse Bay Hotel for the three months with Rosemary and our first two children Julie (aged three) and Graham (eighteen months), the posting came at a solemn time for my family. My beloved father had passed away earlier in the year, when I was away on a trip. His sudden death was understandably a crushing blow for us all and I was brought back immediately to be with the family. As difficult as it was for her, my mother decided she was happy to remain in the family home I grew up in, with her Alsatian dog providing company and keeping her active. Though tough to leave her, by the time we left for Hong Kong she had got into a good routine, and we knew we would not be away too long. For me, it was good to have my family with me, and not be away from them for long stints, as we mourned his loss and the huge gap it left in our hearts and lives.

Despite the difficult timing, we had a memorable time in Hong Kong – vastly different as it was from our first marital home in leafy Ashtead, Surrey. Living in the unique little hotel on an island just the other side of the bay to the airport, the posting afforded us quality time together, and when not travelling to the mainland for shopping trips and sight-seeing, we enjoyed spending time at the hotel pool and on the beach. Soaking up the unique East-meets-West cultural heritage of Hong Kong, we created many early family memories in that short but memorable overseas posting.

Whilst in Hong Kong, my home airport became Kai Tak, which before its closure in 1998 had a special place in the aviation world. With its unusually complex and dramatic approach path through craggy mountains and over Kowloon's skyscrapers to a perilous runway in the middle of a very large bay, it was known as one of the most demanding landings at any airport worldwide. My flight prayer of *"God, please help me today"* was ever present as I navigated the perilous approach, which necessitated the steepest turn in proximity to buildings of any airport in the world, when your wing tip could be within fifty to a hundred yards of one or two of the buildings, so close you could see into people's living rooms. Multiple attempts at landing were not uncommon and while as pilots we enjoyed the challenge, it was no great surprise that the airport had suffered a shocking twelve air disasters in its sixty-two years of operation and was ultimately replaced in 1998 at a cost of USD 20 billion with Hong Kong's new three-runway international airport on the island of Chek Lap Kok.

Once the posting in Hong Kong had run its course, we returned to England, settling into our beautiful family home in Leatherhead overlooking the famous Surrey Hills, and welcomed the addition of our third child Shelley. The work-life balance remained very good to me: my long-haul trips on the 707 interspersed with lengthy periods at home and my career progressing smoothly through the ranks. I embarked on yet more training, becoming an assistant flight instructor on simulators, and enjoyed promotion to 707 Captain in 1971, shortly before turning thirty-eight. That same year saw my further promotion to the 707 fleet management team, which meant that for the first time in my life, when not required to fly, I had a desk job.

In the early years as a pilot I went where I was told, when I was told. A letter would come in the mail, advising me of the latest roster, and off I would go, consequently missing some of the early achievements my children enjoyed. Whilst a slight shock to the system, the upside to "flying a desk" was that it gave me greater control over my schedule. With my advancement to management, I was grateful to be around more and present in my children's day-to-day lives, which was important to me as a young father. It delights me that my daughter Julie remembers that on those occasions when I was not away flying, at bedtime, we would study a map together and I would teach her the locations of different countries and what their capital cities were. Julie recalls knowing some very small countries with relatively unknown capitals thanks to me, many of which she still remembers to this day! Formative years in the life of a ten-, eight- and six-year-old, I got to kick a football or play cricket with my son Graham, or do some maintenance on Julie's bicycle, which she loved as it gave her some much sought-after independence. Playing tennis with Julie and Shelley was a regular endeavour, though it was widely accepted that Rosemary was a far better opponent than I was on the tennis court! Being available to attend sports days, school matches and plays far more frequently during the years that followed was a vital perk of the desk job and one which I tried to make the most of.

Rosemary's love of tennis meant it wasn't long before a court was laid in our garden. Our three young children made the most of our investment, with daughters Julie and Shelley both exhibiting a natural talent from an early age. Whilst our son Graham's tennis skills were a little less remarkable than his sisters', he did enjoy one notable tennis triumph when he was victorious in an Under 12 doubles tournament, and delighted in purchasing his one and only tennis trophy with the 75p winning purse he collected! Regardless of ability, all three children inherited their mother's love of the beautiful game, and Julie led the family tennis charge, paving the way for her younger sister Shelley to follow in her footsteps.

Aside from all the children's activities, Rosemary and I enjoyed an active social life at home; regularly in or out for dinner parties, which often started with a couple of hours of playing bridge. Inevitably the breakfast chat the next morning would include discussions about how good or bad our hands of cards had been, or who had been the target of my latest prank! The cadet japery of my early twenties was still in full flow, and Saturday morning breakfasts was a good time to update the children. Whilst Rosemary might have raised an eyebrow, the children delighted in hearing about my latest wind-up, such as when friends with a certain proclivity for fine wines had come for dinner and I'd decanted a cheap bottle of red wine into the carafe, only to enjoy their subsequent oohing and aahing over its quality! Sunday evenings invariably involved us all gathering in the sitting room to watch something together, before our minds turned to our Monday morning tasks. Whether I was present or off flying, the children always knew that Rosemary was there, providing the stability and consistency that was valued so highly within the family. Weekends were also a good time to visit with my mother, who remained in Ewell. Though she stayed in the main family home for some time after my father's passing, where all those years ago she had encouraged me to pursue Rosemary, my mother eventually moved to a smaller cottage up the road in Ewell. We would visit her regularly until her passing in 1971, sharing as we did the latest chapter in our various family adventures.

Over the years, often at the end of rigorous training or studying sessions, it had been an immense joy for me to share the myriad of lifetime events and successes with my parents, given the keen interest they had always taken in my career. Hearing their own elation and evident pride in my achievements made the highpoints even more memorable. My leave visits home during my RAF days provided the opportunity for more in-depth discussions of my training and what I'd been up to and, thankfully, though my life was rooted in a world in many ways foreign to them, they never tired of hearing all about it. Their interest and support made the hole left by their passing all the more significant, lamenting as I often did, not being able to share my newly scaled milestones with them, a sentiment I felt most keenly when the achievement of Concorde Pilot was added to my licence and I entered the Concorde family.

5

Cleared for Take-off

As 1976 rolled on, there was an excited buzz encircling BA. Having agreed with the UK Government to take possession of seven supersonic Concordes over a period of time, BA needed captains to fly them, and certain captains were being selected for the training. Concorde's reputation was already well known – her performance at twice the speed of sound a great attraction for a pilot such as myself, who had been cruising around eighty per cent of the speed of sound for years in the 707. Already part of the management team of the 707 fleet, I expressed a strong interest in the course and was thrilled to be invited to attend; embarking on yet another in my long list of conversion courses.

Along with other carefully selected pilots, the rigorous training upgraded our skills from the *slower than the speed of sound* subsonic planes of the jumbo era we were hitherto flying, to the more complex supersonic Concorde aircraft. The six-month training course incorporated six weeks of ground school and technical study; eighty hours in a simulator; and three months on Concorde herself.

Most importantly the training involved spending extensive periods of time with the extraordinary Concorde test pilots, Brian Trubshaw and John Cochrane, both remarkable men whose knowledge and experience forever impressed me.

During the course, I spent much time at Filton, towards the Bristol Channel. Residence there was necessary, as a dense schedule of lectures schooled us in the engineering masterpiece, and the simulator tested our supersonic skills. Once those aspects had been completed, we then moved on to *base flying*: repeated take offs and landings. This took place at an airfield close to Filton, and was rapid-fire activity, taking off, then landing all within five minutes, and then repeating the manoeuvre over and over and over again, so it became second nature. This also gave us time to familiarise ourselves with Concorde's nose. The iconic droop nose was not an aesthetic choice but rather pure necessity, designed to enable the flight crew to see the ground during the different phases of her manoeuvres.

Theory sessions taught us that between taxiing, take-off, landing and flight, Concorde's angle relative to the ground was varied, and so too therefore was the captain's ability to see the ground or skies ahead. With the different phases came different nose angles, to facilitate the necessary sight, all of which made more sense during our training and base flying drills. When taxiing, the nose was drooped a few degrees to $5°$ down, to give the captain a view of the taxi way. The same was true for take-off and once airborne and cruising, Concorde's nose returned to the neutral position of $0°$, realigning it with the rest of the airframe as she soared through the skies.

When landing, however, Concorde came in very high – meaning the front of the plane was high and the tail way below the flight line. With such a high position, were the nose to stay at 0°, given the high-pitch angle of the aircraft during the approach, the captain would not be able to see the runway. Even at the 5° down position used for take-off, the view would still not be sufficient, and so for landing, the nose was lowered to 12.5°, thereby giving the captain a perfect view of the runway.

We spent over a week on base flying alone, providing a myriad of different weather conditions and wind strengths for us to get used to handling Concorde, and opportunities for Brian Trubshaw and John Cochrane to share key insights from their vast knowledge of her ways. *Touch and go* was a common feature of those training sessions as well: we would come in for final approach, and when the wheels touched down onto the runway, we would then apply full power again and ascend back into the sky, turn and continue round in a circle and double back for another touchdown landing. The repetitions were endless, but vital if one was to become comfortable handling the beautiful, yet slippery, bird.

I knew the course was going to be demanding. I had been told it was, and knew of the complexities of the aeroplane and that the conversion course from subsonic to supersonic had a twenty-five per cent failure rate, five times higher than that of any other conversion course at BA. Many of the captains who took the course had been flying for over twenty years and were vastly experienced. Understandably, failure was therefore a shattering experience for those who did not pass. For those who managed to stay the course, further handling practice came in the form of the requisite circuit flights, which were conducted at an airfield. Round and round we went, performing circuit after circuit, getting used to the slippery manner in which a mere accidental slip of a finger could send Concorde thundering in an unexpected direction.

In so many ways, the retraining had been like going back into the Air Force, but this time I was in my early forties, married with three children. With thousands of logged flying hours since I first set foot in a Tiger Moth, my schedule reverted to the long nights and weekends of the past. When I wasn't travelling to Filton each week for training, my head was plunged into operational manuals and charts. Rosemary and the children were accustomed to me being away, whether down the road in Filton or the other side of the world in Australia, so my disappearance into my office to study was nothing new. The bins and bills still waited for me, but the regular dinner parties and card games were usually foregone during that time – well, for me at least!

When all the training in the myriad of different manoeuvres had been successfully completed, we progressed to our final test – our passengers. For the safety of all, the first passenger flight was conducted alongside another experienced captain who already had Concorde fleet experience, and was there as a back-up should we need assistance. Once the first of these had been successfully completed, we then began to fly down the BA route to the scheduled destination for Concorde that day. Given

Concorde was at that stage limited as to where she was able to fly, it was not necessarily an Atlantic route we were given. For those who made it to this stage of the process, it would have been very unusual for someone to be rejected, and I certainly was never aware of someone failing at this late juncture. Thankfully, the efforts and sacrifices paid off, and with the successful completion of the training under my belt, it was a wonderful sense of achievement to be signed off by the supervisory captain and cleared for take-off in Concorde. Much like my previous conversion courses had each in turn led on to exciting and challenging new adventures as a pilot, unbeknown to me at the time, the Concorde journey was going to match and far surpass the stimulating exploits I had hitherto enjoyed on the flight deck. I was now on board as a member of the Concorde family and what lay ahead was an even more incredible, supersonic adventure than I could ever have imagined, in more ways than one.

I always remember going to London Heathrow for my first operational flight when I was totally in command, with no senior support captain beside me. The enormity of the responsibility was huge, knowing 109 lives and a £50million aeroplane were in my care. That said, I felt competent and had no doubts about my abilities. With all the training I had received over my years of flying, I trusted that I could measure up to the task before me. The Concorde training had been intense, and I was looking forward to finally completing the task I had committed myself to, of being released into the public sphere as a Concorde Captain.

On a personal level, elevation to Concorde Captain brought changes at home, not just in the form of the many Concorde miniatures I brought home to the children, but also with my travel pattern shifting. No longer was I away for a week or two at a time on long-haul flights, but neither was I back at home for a full week. Flying once a week as I did, I would generally be back mid to late evening on the return flight from New York, and always appreciated returning to the consistency of family life at home, which Rosemary managed with great aplomb. Whilst I was flying across the pond, Rosemary was often travelling between the children's activities, frequenting the professional tennis circuit as Julie and Shelley increasingly made it to the later stages of tournaments. Although I watched when I could, I missed many matches, but always enjoyed hearing about the latest results when I returned home.

Rosemary was equally interested in my "activities", knowing the immense joy I got from flying Concorde, so our evening chats were never dull. On a professional level, when I qualified as a Concorde pilot, Captain Brian Calvert, Technical Manager of Concorde at the time, clocked me on his radar. Noting the experience which I had acquired in the 707 fleet management team, he considered me particularly well suited to his search for an assistant. I was only too glad to join him, but it was to be a short-lived partnership as it was not long after we teamed up that Brian announced he was going back to line flying, assuring me it was to do with the job rather than my arrival!

My further promotion to Technical Manager followed swiftly thereafter and with it came the reality of the

Concorde back office. I was hit head on with the very complex challenges Concorde faced for which there was no quick-fix solution, and it swiftly became abundantly clear that the attitude of British Airways senior management to Concorde was not "will it fail?" but "*when* will it fail?" As far as they were concerned, financial failure was inevitable, not merely because of Concorde's extremely complex engineering but more importantly due to the restrictions on noise levels and supersonic travel at airports and over inhabited land, which vastly limited the potential routes available. For all our belief in the aeroplane, it was hard to see how this could all be resolved with the current status quo.

With such complexities of engineering, failure could have crept up on us in any number of ways, but in 1977 the indisputable principal barrier to success was not technical, but rather the legal battle over the noise pollution Concorde caused when flying into the Big Apple, more commonly known as New York City (NYC). Ultimately, air travel is about getting from one location to another and, given her supersonic speeds, Concorde was unique in this regard. As a Concorde captain, you were flying one of the most beautiful and powerful aircraft to ever take to the skies, with a flight time to New York less than half that of any other passenger aircraft, but this did not happen quietly; Concorde made a lot of noise.

Given the significance of the route, not to be cleared for take-off through NYC would threaten Concorde's very existence, so it was clear to those in the inner sanctum of Concorde operations that we had a fight on our hands.

Consequently, behind the scenes and advancing at an alarming pace was an increasingly turbulent legal, political and commercial climate around Concorde flights. NYC, the most populated city in the US, was the single most critical route for Concorde's commercial success, her only other commercial routes at that stage being Washington, Bahrain and Singapore. Without the New York route, it was believed Concorde would be a commercial disaster, so BA had no option but to fight tooth and nail for access, even if that meant all the way to the US Supreme Court.

Prior to 1977, New Yorkers did not want Concorde flying into their city and had rejected Concorde's request to fly into John F. Kennedy (JFK) Airport. The noise and environmental opposition to her was enormous and had ensured that we had not been allowed anywhere near NYC, or the heavily populated surrounding areas. However, following intensive lobbying by British Airways, the Port of New York Authority finally granted us permission to demonstrate that Concorde could meet the noise requirements of JFK. The challenge was on and I wasted no time joining forces with the noise reduction experts at British Aerospace. Our aim, which our many detractors thought impossible, was to devise a procedure whereby Concorde could take off without violating the very strict noise monitoring that the New York authorities had for every runway at the airport. The consequences were stark – if we couldn't deliver then Concorde was in jeopardy. This was in every respect a joint issue for both British Airways and Air France, the New York route being equally vital to Concorde's survival for both. As such, the preparation necessitated close co-operation between the two airlines.

As Technical Manager of the BA Concorde fleet, I was responsible for BA's response and during the following few months I spent a lot of time brain storming with Concorde's manufacturers, working on the best way to achieve noise abatement in each of the different stages of the take-off, and then translating our findings into something that could be done repeatedly. Everything had to be analysed, from how we would best get into the air; what stage we would throttle back; and which way we would immediately turn, depending on the runway and the degrees of bank we would employ. No area was ignored and I spent many hours at JFK reviewing their runways, scrutinising each of them and the options available on any given route. Weeks of our preparation time went into the theory of how to handle the plane and what to do when we took off from a particular runway. Once that had all been calculated, we transferred to the simulator for practice and refining of the plan.

The meticulous preparation resulted in a procedure which, according to my calculations, would minimise the noise of the plane and therefore hopefully add New York City to Concorde's destinations. With the planning phase complete, I travelled to Toulouse where the French had been preparing a Concorde ready for the New York test flight. Several days prior to our departure from Toulouse for New York, we received a comprehensive briefing from the Air France PR and legal teams about the hostile greeting we could expect to receive on our arrival. In excess of 100 journalists were following the Concorde story and I was acutely aware of the animosity towards allowing Concorde into JFK from various press articles I had seen and radio broadcasts I had heard. A *New York Times* story from 9th March 1977 attests quite bluntly to the sentiments of the time, asserting that Concorde was a *"commercial corpse"*, the journalist writing that *"the Governments of Britain, France and even the United States have tried to dump the body on New York's doorstep – Kennedy Airport to be exact. The sanity of the Western alliance, nay, the fate of democracy in Europe, are said to depend on half a million residents of Queens putting up with the plane's extraordinary take-off roar and rumble. How shall New York cope with the Concorde? A decision is in order in the next few weeks"*.[1] An extreme position taken by the journalist, but nonetheless an honest depiction of the sentiments we were facing and the challenge we had to overcome.

Flying under the captaincy of my French counterpart Jean Franchi, the plane and plan prepared, we took off from Toulouse and flew supersonic, heading for JFK Airport in New York City. From an altitude of 2,000 feet, through a gauntlet of light aircraft and helicopters all positioned to catch a glimpse of Concorde with cameras snapping at breakneck speed, we entered the final approach. The runway area was crammed with crowds of onlookers, and as we came in to land I recorded just three words on my Dictaphone: *"This is history."* Those three simple words

---

1. https://www.nytimes.com/1977/03/09/archives/the-battle-of-concorde.html

summed up the significance of the occasion, for me personally, but also for Jean Franchi and me as pilots, for our airlines, for supersonic travel and for aviation history. It was huge.

Once landed, we were ushered to a press conference held in a large hangar, allowing ample room for the multitude of journalists waiting for us. With the vitriolic barrage of full-on media onslaught hurled directly at us, it was more a "press attack" than a press conference. Whilst the panel consisted of representatives from Air France, British Aerospace and BA, of which I was one representative, the majority of the questions were aimed at me personally, the French having conveniently decided that the language barrier was likely to be insurmountable for them to provide adequate responses. *"Captain Walpole, how long will it take you to deafen our children with that aeroplane of yours? Captain Walpole, how long before the windows are shattered in the surrounding countryside? Captain Walpole ...? Captain Walpole ...?"* The questions were never-ending, in pursuit of headlines more than rational answers, and came thick and fast, often not even allowing time for me to start, let alone complete my response.

Just as the hostility was at its peak and tempers ran the risk of erupting, a truly extraordinary event occurred. With the noise of the hangar doors being hauled open, all heads turned to witness Concorde being towed in. The place fell silent at the sight of the magnificent aircraft; the atmosphere transformed as unfettered vitriol turned to appreciation of this streamlined beauty, and the awe and wonder she inspired. In that instant, the winds changed and our course shifted. Accusations turned to curiosity; anger turned to admiration; cautious self-defence turned to welcome pride in our day job; and a sense of hope came over the team. It was a game changer, the start of what was to be a momentous few days, and the precursor to a whole new chapter in the Concorde journey.

Having survived the somewhat spicy appetizer of the press conference, our focus turned to the main course – the New York Port Authority, who would be the real arbiters of Concorde's fate. It was clear to me that they did not believe we could operate within their criteria, and the eleventh-hour stipulation that we carry greater ballast to ensure a take-off weight fully representative of a transatlantic departure, rendered our task no easier and their doubt more justified. Put simply, the greater the take-off weight the slower the climb, and consequently the longer we would be nearer to the noise monitors on the ground, and the myriad of homes in New York waiting to see if the vibrations caused by Concorde's rumble would knock their carefully hung wall pictures off their fixings. Unbeknownst to me, the extra ballast had apparently always been part of their test criteria, but our last-minute awareness of the stipulation had a significant impact on our prepared flight calculations and we had limited time to make the necessary modifications and adapt the plan. Experienced at operating under fast-paced and stressful circumstances, we made the changes in time and the following day would be the moment of truth. We did not have long to wait.

Staying in the same hotel, the crew had a comprehensive briefing in the morning and then we boarded our transport which would take us to the plane. As we made our way to the runway, if by that point in my life I had given the power of God any credibility, that would surely have been the moment for fervent authentic prayer, silent or otherwise. Instead, what I knew was to trust the hours of preparation, planning and tireless input of the many brilliant minds of our team, and hope that it would all come good and deliver the only result we could dare contemplate. I do, however, distinctly remember as I travelled out to JFK, alongside Jean Franchi in the transport bus, with my little John's Gospel safely tucked in my case, that I again uttered my traditional flight prayer of *"God, please help us today."* It was not that I considered myself a man of faith, but I knew the significance of what we were about to do, and I was not about to change what had become a regular habit for me during my flying career.

This was to be the first ever take off for Concorde *out* of New York and it was on *my* watch. Under the attentive gaze of the Statue of Liberty, as the battle for Concorde's future came to its climax, I would captain the flight which would determine history. I remember taxiing out and thinking, *"The future of Concorde is at stake here, I categorically cannot get this wrong."* The plan was quite a complicated manoeuvre, involving getting airborne, throttling the engines back and then reapplying power all at exactly the right time, and the pressure was intense. With noise-measuring equipment everywhere we looked, Concorde's first and potentially last take-off out of JFK was finally in motion.

With meticulous precision, I executed our carefully devised take-off procedure from Runway 31L, lifting off to fifty feet, completing a 25° left bank before throttling back (reducing power) at a predetermined number of seconds from take-off, to the scrupulously calculated engine power. Rolling off the bank, we kept climbing at exactly 250 knots, turned and then we were clear of the monitors. The specific combination was our designed plan to ensure noise levels were low enough to meet the requirements for NYC, whilst allowing enough power to take off safely. For all the perceived perfection in our execution, seated as we were in the flight deck we had no means of knowing whether we had succeeded and achieved the necessary target.

Up to that point I was too focused on the task at hand to have allowed any room for emotions, positive or negative. However, having been told before we left, *"If you have time, call us up, and we'll let you know the results,"* heart in my mouth, I got on the radio and requested feedback on our take off. The response was thunderous and could have been taken from one of Hollywood's finest scripts: *"Brian, congratulations, you did not even trigger the monitor."* Incredible. Astounding. Phenomenal. Extraordinary. Historic. Mind-blowing. Miraculous. Words cannot do justice to the emotions which coursed through my veins that day. Having devised and practised the procedure over many weeks, to then transfer it to reality and perform the manoeuvre in the test flight, and the plan come together and successfully achieve the goal, was, to say the least, an immense relief. Grateful that it had all worked as planned, at the same time I felt a huge sense of achievement that all the late nights and refining had paid off. We had silenced our detractors and succeeded in what was considered by many to be the impossible. My heart was still in my mouth, but it was different. No more anxious anticipation and the destiny of an aircraft on my shoulders. We had fought for New York and had won, and she was finally cleared for take-off from NYC.

I remember as we taxied in being greeted by crowds of people waving and cheering; shouts of well-done rebounding off the walls as we entered the terminal; and huge smiles and grins on the faces of the gathered BA management who added their own commendations of "Brilliantly done, Brian." Coming from them, it meant a lot. If we had made a mistake in this demonstration flight, the extent to which Concorde would have been inhibited would likely have been insurmountable. Yes, we could have requested a re-run, but there was no guarantee it would have been granted, or that other legal objections would not have thwarted our efforts. All those thoughts and concerns were now redundant. We had succeeded. We had answered the critics and doubters and Concorde would live to fly many more days into New York City; a future reality we did not have to wait long to see come to fruition.

On 22nd November 1977, forty days before my forty-fourth birthday, Concorde was cleared for the first ever commercial flight from Heathrow to JFK. I had the honour of captaining that flight: yet another first the beautiful bird and I shared during my tenure. My son, who was fifteen at the time and at boarding school, was allowed by the House Master into Matron's room to watch the 9 o'clock news that night, which was headlined by elated reports of the flight. His immense excitement and pride that his father was the captain was shared enthusiastically by those watching with him. It was a historic day for aviation; a globally televised and much headlined event; and most certainly of great pride for me, my family, our team and the entire Concorde family as Concorde began a whole new chapter of her journey.

6

An Unexpected Journey

Flying from London to JFK at 10.30am was a routine I came to know well. Leaving home around 8am in my uniform, I would drive to Heathrow and, more often than not, go through the emergency drills, checklists, what to do if x or y happens, revising them in my head as I made my way to the BA HQ building where officers would meet. After rendezvousing with other crew members, a BA bus would pick us up and transport us to the Operations (ops) Control in the centre of the airport. What followed was a briefing for the captain and co-pilot by the flight ops staff, which included our flight plan with expected flight time, fuel requirement based on weight and weather forecast for our route. As part of our planning, we would also discuss an alternative landing destination, and the weather that was expected there and how much fuel would be required should we need to divert. If fog was too thick for us to land at our scheduled destination, for example, diversion would be necessary. As Captain, based on the information presented, I would decide how many extra kilos of fuel we would load. During the comprehensive briefing, the flight ops staff would present other calculations, such as where we could land in the event of engine failure, the idea being we always have a solution prepared, so that whatever problem befell us, we would have a plan of action. As we became more experienced with Concorde and her subtle nuances, the plans matured and were comprehensively updated.

With decisions made, depending on the location of the Concorde, the captain and co-pilot were then either driven out to the aircraft or we walked with our briefcase to the stairs. Once on board, I would always take off my hat and jacket and hang them on the little rail behind the door of the flight deck. Climbing into our seats, we began the various checks of our instruments. The captain and co-pilot both had their own set of instruments and dials in front of them, reason being, that in the event that instruments failed, you had one on the other set of dials. The duplication of dials also meant that the aircraft could always be flown from either the captain's *or* co-pilot's seat. With the physical checklist in hand, the engineer or co-pilot would read each one out loud, whilst both the captain and co-pilot checked their instruments. Checks ranged from setting the altimeter and air speed, to "V1 stop go" and speed dials, and when completed, we would respond "checked". During take-off, the point in time and distance by which the aeroplane can come to a halt within the remaining runway available is known as V1. Suffice to say, V1 was not something you wanted to practise – the brakes would be burnt out and welded onto the plates. Nevertheless, if one ever needed to abandon a flight before reaching V1, to help stop we would slam the throttles closed, select reverse on the engines and engage the brakes. However, once you have passed V1, the plane has to take off, as if it tried to stop, the time and length of runway needed to do so would be insufficient (you would not have time to stop in the length of the runway remaining) and it would likely crash.

With the checks all complete, we were then ready to ask for *start-up permission* from Air Traffic Control (ATC), who when ready would inform us that we were "clear to start". If the captain was flying the aircraft, the co-pilot would conduct the radio comms with ATC, and vice versa, and once cleared, the next set of checks for *starting the engines* would then commence. Unbeknownst to many, there is a procedure called "lighting up the engine igniters" which is required before the engines start. The engine igniters are required to power up equipment which is needed for turning the engines. As the igniters are lit, a ground engineer watches, ensuring they are "turning over" and nothing untoward is happening externally. Once all are turning, the ground power unit attached to the aircraft to help start the engines is taken away and it is then clear for starting the engines. One at a time, all four engines are started in order, going across the wing from one to four. Once all four engines were running, we would then be back on the radio to ATC requesting taxi clearance, and once received we would be ready to taxi out slowly. You cannot reverse an aircraft on its power, so a tractor is required to push you back from the gate, and the ground crew would be on the radio saying, *"Brake release now please,*

Captain," so that the tractor could push us back. Once the aircraft was ready to taxi, the ground staff would detach the tractor from the plane and message that we were all clear, which would trigger a further radio to ATC from the flight deck, requesting taxi clearance.

As we taxied out, another instrument check would have us checking that all the dials were appropriately set, and would come before one of the most detailed and comprehensive checklists – *the take-off*. Again, we were checking the instruments in front of us, including airspeed and V1 rotations, as well as a myriad of variable positions which were on the edge of the instruments. Taxiing was always very controlled in a stage-by-stage process, requiring confirmation from ATC before you progressed to the next stage. With a very long aircraft moving around the runway, it was vital to manage the process in order to make sure we did not get into a position where we should not be. Afterall, if Concorde needed to reverse, she could not, and so would begin a ripple effect delay on the entire airport as a tractor would need to be deployed to assist!

As we approached the runway, ATC were watching and would be in regular communications, advising that we were at first only clear to the holding point and not onto the runway. Once at the holding point, we would hold and tell them we were "*ready to go*", at which point ATC may say something like, "*We've got one landing, and you're clear to line up after he's on the ground.*" Having lined up on the runway, ATC would then inform us, "*You're clear to go,*" and so it began. Opening the throttles, we released the brakes and started the stop watch on our instrument panel! Perhaps not what you expected to hear for such a sophisticated aircraft, but the stop watch was important as it related to the noise abatement restrictions we were operating under. With a specific time set for reduction of power, it was vital we did not exceed the limit, to ensure the impact of the roaring noise of take-off was minimised for the benefit of the residents below. The stop watch setting would vary, depending on the weight of the aircraft, as did the V1 speed, and both having set our stop watches on the instrument panel, we began our acceleration. The co-pilot continued calling out the various readings, such as air speed building, our speed in knots, V1, and so it went on.

Key to take off were Concorde's famous afterburners, which burned vast amounts of fuel while reheating the exhaust gases after combustion to increase the thrust. Facilitating pure acceleration, the initial impact was fantastic – pressed back into your seat, even when the aircraft was heavy for a trans-Atlantic flight, it really was an extreme exhibition of power. Of course, we were strapped in and our seats were secure, but you were still very aware that acceleration was incredibly swift. With a steady roar rumbling through the aircraft, and eyes on the airspeed indicator winding up, the aircraft would smoothly take off. When our stop watches reached the predetermined point, we would pull back on the power and continue to climb. Once airborne, and with autopilot engaged leaving our hands free for the constant review of the instrument settings, ATC would clear the flight to climb to a height such as 5,000 feet. ATC were responsible for the separation of our aircraft from all other aircraft which were either coming in to land or flying over the airfield as we were taking off, so we progressed incrementally. Having reached the next height they had cleared us to, we would level off and radio in to tell them, *"Speedbird at 10,000 feet"* (Speedbird being the BA callsign for Concorde), to which they would reply, *"Roger, we'll clear you higher."*

Reapplying power, we continued to climb and at various stages in the climb we would be handed from one area of ATC to another. This incremental process would continue, steadily clearing us from one height to the next. As we reached circa 30,000 feet, we were usually given a new radio frequency as we came into another control area. Flying subsonic circa 500/600mph (0.9 the speed of sound) out towards the west coast of Britain, once over the water we would request clearance to *accelerate and climb*. With clearance duly granted, we would relight the afterburners and initiate our climb and acceleration. Feeling the tilt on your back, we would accelerate and climb until we reached Mach 2, and as the aircraft decreased in weight due to the burn off of fuel, we would gradually creep up in altitude. Though we reached great heights as the aircraft decreased in weight through fuel burn, the cruising altitude was forever changing. Constantly monitoring the dials, checking our fuel burn, making sure, for example, that the computers were correctly programmed and taking us in the right direction, monitoring the weight of the aircraft, the weather at our destination as well as Boston (in the event we needed to divert or had engine failure), our job never stopped. This is why flying Concorde was not just physically tiring but also far more mentally draining than flying a 707, despite it being a shorter flight. Though we were always busy, once we were out over the Atlantic, we still tried to make time for visits to the flight deck, albeit for a brief moment!

Unless asked to deviate by ATC, such as for military aircraft in the skies, there was a standard route for Concorde across the Atlantic. Nevertheless, the ops team at BA would still file the flight plan with ATC so they had confirmation of our route. That said, while out over the Atlantic, we would check in every 10 degrees west with ATC, telling them where we were with messages such as *"Speedbird 1 is at 20 west 50,000 feet"* and so it would continue until we got to 50 degrees west, close to the American east coast. One of the joys of flying supersonic is it is just you up there at 55,000-60,000 feet, as there were no flight routes which had Concorde passing each other, unless, of course, it was a photo shoot with BA's photographer Adrian Meredith! However, as we got closer to deceleration and descent, we would be handed over to US east coast ATC in New York or Canada, who were handling the busy traffic of the north Atlantic subsonic route. Tuning into their VHF frequency, we gave our position and requested descent clearance, and so began the reverse of our ascent, descending to 50,000 then 40,000 feet, slowing our speed to subsonic as we continued to make sure we did not send a "boom carpet" over the inhabited coast. Oft maligned for her noise if flying supersonic, what people on the ground would suddenly hear when Concorde sped across the skies was a blanket of noise, known as the "boom carpet". The supersonic boom carpet stretched about twenty-five miles either side of the aircraft, and in front of it. The boom itself was not frightening, but rather it was the suddenness of the bang, with no forewarning. Such was the importance of not imposing the boom on the inhabitants below, the deceleration-point would be on our map and computer and part of another of our vital in-flight checklists. As we returned to subsonic, we entered into the normal operating height for all subsonic jets flying across the Atlantic. In our deceleration descent, we were cleared down along the coast and as we approached New York, ATC would clear us to 15,000 feet, then 10,000 feet. Soon we were handed over to Kennedy ATC, who would clear us to 5,000 feet, and specify a speed for us as we approached the airport.

As we closed in on the airport, the *approach checklist* was our next job, swiftly followed by the *landing gear checklist*. More often than not, we would have a manual landing. Afterall, pilots want to fly (!!). With the landing gear down and the undercarriage green lights on, my left hand would be on the control column and right hand on the throttles. Coming in to land, the nose would be down and we would endeavour to execute a lovely touch down, greasing the wheels onto the runway. The nose wheel was next onto the tarmac, after which we would select full reverse on the engines along with the brakes, and between them they would decelerate the aircraft rapidly. Once landed, preferably without having thumped the aircraft down on the ground, there was still work to do. With the nose raised to its taxiing position, still under ATC, we would be cleared to taxi to our parking bay and the ground crew would guide us in. With the stairs put into position at the front door, while the flight engineer went through the *shutdown checklist*, I would usually be out of my seat ready to bid our passengers au revoir, never missing an opportunity to remind them that they had crossed the Atlantic in three hours twenty-three minutes! With hat, briefcase and jacket gathered, I would not be far behind the passengers as they made their way to passport control. Whilst as crew we did not have to queue, we still had to go through the official controls, and would then join our baggage which the ground crew usually put on the BA transport for us. With our job for the day complete, our next destination was the hotel.

The alpha and omega of my flying career could not have been more contrasting – from the twin-seated single-engine Tiger Moth biplane where it all began, to the Rolls Royce Olympus turbo jet engines of supersonic Concorde where my career reached its pinnacle, they were worlds apart. The same could be said for another aspect of my life – faith. Though the little John's Gospel had transferred from the pocket in my RAF flight suit to my BA briefcase, faith didn't really feature with any significance on the radar of my life until, that is, a tennis dinner in 1981. Rosemary and I were attending with our youngest daughter Shelley, whose tennis achievements meant she was up for an award, and what happened that night set in motion a chain of events which were to be the catalyst for an entirely unexpected journey for us all.

Shelley was fifteen at the time, and considered by some a rising tennis star, going on as she did to win the British Junior Hardcourt Championships three times. A gentleman by the name of Gerald Williams, a renowned British tennis commentator and journalist, had been following Shelley's progress. He was in attendance at the dinner that evening and made a point of coming over to speak to Rosemary and me at our table. Reflecting on what a great player and person Shelley was, Gerald happened to mention he was heading to New York later in the week to commentate on an upcoming tournament in the tennis calendar. Cheekily, I asked Gerald how he was getting there, and commiserated with him when he responded that he'd be at the back of a 747!

The timing could not have been more perfect. I was flying to New York the same day as Gerald, and at the time was also responsible for the commercial activity of Concorde. With the ever-whirring marketing side of my brain piqued, I made Gerald a proposition: *"Gerald, I'll put you on my Concorde to New York provided that you undertake, when sitting in front of your microphone, to wax lyrical about your flight on Concorde to the tennis fans you'll be reaching, far and wide, during your commentary."* Gerald barely missed a beat before accepting my offer, the seats of Concorde posing far greater appeal than the rear end of a 747. It was a win-win, and I was hopeful that some much-needed positive publicity would be forthcoming in Concorde's direction. Being at the height of Concorde's money bleed, we were in need of all the marketing exposure we could muster. While hopeful of what this might generate, I had little grasp at the time of the full impact that this request would have on me personally. Moreover, I also hadn't bargained for the full extent of Gerald's gifting as a salesman, but I didn't have to wait long to find out.

After thoroughly enjoying his supersonic flight to New York, Gerald was preparing to disembark when he turned to me and expressed his genuine and heartfelt appreciation. Assuming he would then continue on his way, I was somewhat surprised when he requested I do him the kindness of having breakfast with him the next day. Knowing my diary was clear, I was only too happy to accept his invitation and accordingly met him the next morning in the hotel and enjoyed one of New York's finest breakfast offerings. After we had eaten, noting as he had that I *"seemed to have everything"*, Gerald candidly enquired as to what part God played in my life. I didn't realise that Gerald was a Christian, and though his comment caught me a little off guard, my honest response of *"none"* didn't seem to surprise him in the slightest, and he promptly issued a second invitation, this one a little more challenging than the first. Simply put, Gerald asked me if I'd like to join him at his church in Guildford one Sunday after a spot of tea, once he had completed his work in the US and returned to England.

Rosemary and I enjoyed an active social life, often hosting events, and I have always enjoyed the opportunity to meet new people at events. That said, since my interactions with the chaplain at Tiger Squadron, and whilst still carrying my little John's Gospel with me, I had not progressed beyond that in terms of church life and faith. Understandably, still very much the "church for weddings and funerals" type of man that I was, the idea of Gerald's invitation of "tea with the vicar" was less than appealing, so when he asked me if I would like to join him, I politely answered, *"Not particularly, no!"* For anyone who knew Gerald, it will come as no surprise that this did not deter him one bit. Reminding me that he would be making all the right noises for me about Concorde in his commentary over the next few weeks, despite the fact that thanks to me he'd just crossed the Atlantic in speedy and luxurious fashion, he still asked me to join him for tea as *a favour to him*! Though I had far more than a hint of hesitation, something inside me sensed I should say yes, and I reluctantly agreed to a cautious *"Maybe"*. Returning to London shortly thereafter, I didn't hear from Gerald for some time; no doubt subconsciously I was somewhat relieved to think I had dodged the church visit.

By what, at the time, seemed to be sheer coincidence, suddenly Gerald was back on the scene, and still as insistent as ever about his invitation to church. Barely before we'd even said hello, the dulcet tones of Gerald's *"Come on, Brian"* were encouraging me to join him. Whilst my primary thought was *Oh no*, something in me said yes, and we set a date and agreed to meet for tea beforehand; not surprisingly, Gerald had a plan! Blended into our very English tea was a thorough briefing from Gerald about going to church at Guildford Baptist Church in Millmead: *"Brian,"* he began, *"before we go on to my church, I must prepare you in a modest way. You will never have seen anything quite like this before. There will be several hundred people, a band and an enigmatic pastor called Bob Roxburgh who won't be wearing a dog collar. I just want you to sit and absorb what you see and hear."*

Despite his supposed reassurances causing my mounting reservations to soar to Concorde heights, the lack of dog collar sounded quite intriguing and I determined to keep an open mind and, per Gerald's instruction, to listen to what I heard. The service proved equal to Gerald's briefing and though quite the novel experience to be a passenger in proceedings, to my astonishment I was actually highly impressed with what I witnessed and experienced in the service that day. The complete involvement and unconditional commitment of everyone present, all immersed, with animated faces, listening to the Bible being read and taught, cheerful in their worship and praying openly, was a pleasant novelty to witness. Perhaps to my own surprise, if not Gerald's, I left thinking I might even like to return. A seed had certainly been sown, and a different set of wheels were now turning.

I did indeed return to Millmead, several Sundays in a row in fact, and on one occasion suggested to Rosemary that she might like to join me. Despite the same lack of interest that I had initially displayed, she humoured me and came along on the odd occasion, but was not enthusiastic about returning. The more frequent my attendance, the stronger my relationship with the assistant pastor became; a lovely man called Justin Dennison. Our friendship was further enhanced by our common love of squash and many competitive hours were regularly sweated out on the court at a local club, after which we would go to the bar for a beer and sandwich. Inevitably our conversations would circle back to faith, with Justin often telling me about upcoming events at church, or lending me a book to help answer one of the many questions I had showered him with. I valued those times and the ease with which he allowed me to investigate the Christian faith over a beer, and my esteem for him rose ever further when, sometime later, Justin told me that he didn't actually even drink!

Over the many months of my journey, Justin lent me various books, helped answer the difficult questions of a probing enquirer and consistently pointed me to the Bible for answers. He nurtured me spiritually during what you might call yet another in my long list of *conversion* courses. One particular book he lent me was Josh McDowell's investigative look at faith called *Evidence that Demands a Verdict*. To be frank, calling it a book is slightly misleading: it is more of an encyclopaedia of deep-dive analysis into the credibility of the Christian faith, penned using a compilation of notes written in preparation for a lecture series of his, titled "Christianity: Hoax or History?". With chapter headings ranging from "Archaeology and Biblical Criticism" to "If Jesus Wasn't God, He Deserves an Oscar", to say the analysis is far reaching, would be an understatement. One particularly popular eye-catching chapter is "Significance of Deity: The Trilemma – Lord, Liar or Lunatic", which looked at the opinion that *"If the New Testament records about Jesus are historically accurate, there remain only three logical choices concerning*

Being interviewed by Graham Lacey for the TBN Special about my life as Captain Concorde

In the Captain's Seat, like the one Graham Lacey purchased

*Concorde gave her passengers a magnificent view
of the curvature of the earth*

With my mother and baby brother Colin 1936 and smartly attired with Colin 1938

As an RAF pilot

Year		AIRCRAFT		Pilot, or 1st Pilot	2nd Pilot, Pupil or Passenger
1952		Type	No.		
Month	Date				
—	—	—	—	—	—
JUNE	24	DH 82 A.	S124/25	Mᴿ BARKER.	SELF.
"	"	"	"	"	"
			"	"	"

First flight log book entry June 1952

RAF days, standing on the wing of a Chipmunk 1952

Flanked by fellow trainees on the Ox Box 1953

Earning my Wings late 1953

*Celebrating my 21st birthday
in 1955 with my parents at
Cuddington Golf Club*

*Formation Aerobatics with
Tiger Squadron 1955 (Meteors)*

*In 1955 with my motoring pride
and joy, my Austin Healey*

*With Rosemary at our wedding,
31st January 1959*

Enjoying my time as a first officer on a Boeing 707, 1961

With all the family on holiday in Cape Cod in 1967

Concorde taking off, with her droop nose providing full visibility of the runway. The BA photographer, Adrian Meredith, was lying at the end of the runway to take this picture, and could feel the heat from the afterburners on the back of his neck as Concorde took to the skies

One of the early WWI versions of the little John's Gospel, which I carried around with me. I came to understand, as it said inside, that what the compass and instruments are to the naval officer and the ordnance map is to the field officer, so the Bible is to us in our journey through life

My smile concealing the pressure I was under at the press conference the day before the noise monitoring at JFK in 1977, which would determine the fate of Concorde

The Mach Meter showing Mach 2

A new era began as Concorde was cleared to fly into JFK

The Queen & Prince Philip waving at us from the deck of the Royal Yacht Britannia near Barbados on the 1977 Silver Jubilee Tour

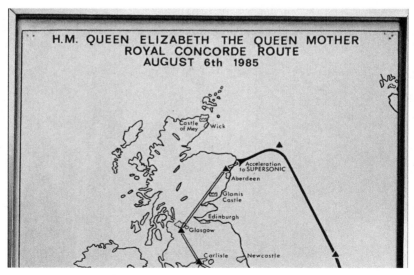

The flight for the Queen Mother in celebration of her 85th birthday included accelerating to supersonic north of Aberdeen

*The Queen Mother was allowed more time
than most in the Jump Seat*

Bidding the Queen Mother farewell, after her Birthday flight

Concorde's tenth anniversary celebrations – Christmas Eve 1985.
Formation flying reminiscent of my RAF days

The four abreast echelon formation, as shown on the cover,
this time photographed from above

The swan formation

The diamond formation

With the Prince and Princess of Wales at the opening of the Concorde lounge at Heathrow Terminal 4 – 1st April 1986

CANADA:

PROVINCE OF BRITISH COLUMBIA:

I, Captain Brian Walpole

of   British Airways Pilot
         (Occupation)

understand that it is alleged that I have committed (

1). Speeding within a sky-way.
2). Fail to wear seatbelt.
3). No tail-lights
4). Fail to signal on turn.
5). Inadequate mufflers.

The speeding ticket issued by the Royal Canadian Mounted Police August 1986 following our low-level flying over the City of Toronto on the way to the 1986 Toronto Air Show

In Toronto for the 1986 Air Show with First Officers John Piper and Jock Lowe and engineer Terry Quarrey

Flying Prime Minister Margaret Thatcher to Vancouver in July 1986 for World Expo – her first Concorde flight

An artist's impression of Concorde Barrel Rolling

21st September 1987, the European Ryder Cup Captain Tony Jacklin thought the safest place for the Ryder Cup was the flight deck, and left it with us for the duration of the flight

With Rosemary, Graham and Shelley at
Buckingham Palace receiving my OBE in 1988

With the children and grandchildren celebrating Rosemary's
80th birthday at Tregenna Castle Cornwall, April 2017

With my loyal and faithful friend Zephyr

His identity."[2] An oft-used discussion point, this was originally made by the author C.S. Lewis who went on to say, *"Christianity, if false, is of no importance, and if true, of infinite importance, the only thing it cannot be is moderately important."*[3]

A wealth of analysis explaining how Christianity is a fact-based faith, *Evidence that Demands a Verdict* deals head on with a myriad of arguments which have been used for disbelieving the Christian faith. For my analytical scientific mind, alongside the Bible, this book proved to be one of the most helpful and convincing books in my exploration and faith growth; one of the pivotal beliefs he explained so clearly being that there was life after the life we know here on earth. This rang true for me; maybe all those hours staring across the celestial creation in Concorde's cockpit were finally beginning to make more sense. The pieces of the puzzle were taking shape and I realised that I was no longer arguing with his responses in my head. Furthermore, I actually thought there was credibility in his explanations. So it was, aged forty-seven, I began a new, far more incredible journey than any I had enjoyed in the ethereal skies above.

Perhaps the incident with Gerald should not really have come as such a surprise. Though unexpected, there were many aspects to it that made sense, not least the tennis part. Indeed, tennis was a central part of family life at that stage. The children were mid-teens to early twenties, and

---

2. *The New Evidence that Demands a Verdict*, Josh McDowell, page viii
3. https://www.goodreads.com/quotes/26465 accessed 5th June 2024

where possible I tried to manage my diary around the various tournaments and activities which they were all participating in. Graham was busy studying at Cambridge, whilst Julie and Shelley were constantly competing in tennis tournaments, and Rosemary and I travelled all over the country watching each of them. I am not sure I helped much, especially during the close matches, as I got incredibly nervous and would be continually pacing around, standing behind trees, unable to sit still. One such trip was to Eastbourne, where we travelled every summer for the National Grass Court Championships at Devonshire Park. I recall one match circa 1981/82, which I spent hiding in a tree as Shelley was playing in the final of her age group against Vanessa Binns; the ebbs and flows of the match wreaking havoc on my nerves. Round the world flying with perilous runways, I was stoic, but like many parents over the years, the angst of watching your children play sport was a whole other level of angst.

A different kind of family anxiety was endured by us all when it came to family holidays. As a BA pilot, I enjoyed the privilege embraced by many employees, of my family having access to free or discounted BA flights, should seats be available. We were therefore able to go to some exotic places at a relatively low cost. Given the distances, this usually meant we were heading off for two weeks, and so there was a lot riding on those flights. Whilst there was no guarantee a seat would be free, knowing which days of the week were more likely to experience fuller loads (capacity), Rosemary and I would plan our holidays and hope! As many people experience, flying "standby" can be nerve-wracking at the best of times when it's just one of you. You make your plans, book your accommodation and possibly hire a car at the other end, pack and hope there will be one seat for you. Doing this for five people, three of whom were children, was another level.

My son reminds me of the methodical contingency planning which took place every time we travelled to the airport. *"If there are only two seats then Mum and this child can get on but if three of us can get on, then this is what we will do . . ."* and so it went on. Whilst the others may have had reason to be more concerned and were often quite anxious on the journey to the airport, a combination of my knowledge of flying patterns and the many relationships I had developed, meant I was usually fairly confident of the entire family having seat belts fastened for our latest adventure. Thankfully we never had to leave anyone behind and our much-appreciated flight was usually followed by two wonderful uninterrupted weeks together, where I was able to be fully present as a father and husband.

Time with my family always meant more to me than I probably articulated enough. I was, and still am, a stickler for punctuality, discipline and order, and though I no doubt told them to go back to bed, deep down I still quietly loved it when one of the children, unable to sleep, would come downstairs and snuggle in my lap. It has been one of my greatest achievements to parent our children, and that they so often came to me over the years with their problems, and I was able to help ease their angst, was a cherished pleasure. That they saw me as their safe place was a reward I did not earn, but have cherished nonetheless.

My daughter Shelley recalls a special game I used to play with them around bedtime, when they were young, called "Magic Dice". Following much pleading, on their part, all three children would gather in the bedroom and the game would commence. The basic premise was I pretended to throw dice out of a bedroom window at night time and then would discreetly hide it somewhere in the room and they had to find it. For years, the children believed that I did actually throw the dice out of the window, and that the dice magically made the journey back into the room on its own volition, and hid. The excitement of young minds wowed by their father's magical skill was a joy, and lasted a number of years, until that is, they grew up and realised my deft of hand! That said, I was not always so skilful, and am reminded of one rather unfortunate instance when I failed to hold onto the dice when hurling my hand towards the window, pretending to eject it into the garden. The subsequent flying dice journeying at pace towards the pane of glass, and resultant smashed window, to this day puts a wry smile on their faces – the delight at their meticulously disciplined and competitive father making such a faux pas delighting them (and subsequently their own children) a little more than I care to admit!

7

Fasten Your Seatbelts

For all the technical successes that we enjoyed in New York on the historical first flight and the excitement they generated, there was no escaping the fact that back at London Heathrow's Speedbird House (the office block which housed BA's headquarters), Concorde remained very much under the commercial microscope. The journalists' derogatory *"commercial corpse"* narrative was far too accurate for comfort, as Concorde was experiencing substantial and unsustainable operational losses; further explaining why I had asked Gerald Williams for some favourable PR. As a team we were constantly seeking ways in which the service could be improved, and I lost count of the number of letters I sent to the BA Board outlining my proposals. Supported by much lobbying from influential colleagues, not least BA's own Planning Director Keith Wilkins, who became a great ally, I continued sending letters reinforcing the need as I saw it for Concorde to have its own dedicated team. To my huge surprise, the letters were not sent in vain, and in 1982, six years after taking on the role of Technical Manager, my secretary informed me that I had been summoned by Lord King, the BA Chairman.

As I entered his office, Lord King was seated at his desk and I stood before him, no doubt resembling my attention stance of RAF yesteryear. Wasting no time in delivering his message, he began ... *"Captain Walpole, I'm going to give you the opportunity to put your money where your mouth has been for the last few years – I'm going to form a Concorde division which will be your responsibility. Concorde has been bleeding British Airways dry, losing millions every year and I will give you two years in which to turn it around. You will form your own team, operate as an airline within an airline, and you will become General Manager. It is down to you."* There was little discussion after that – his thoughts were clear and my bluff had clearly been called. The myriad of proposals and improvements I had suggested to improve commercial viability and stem the financial bleed were now on my head to deliver.

"It is down to you" – his words ringing in my ear, I knew when I walked out of his office that if we didn't turn it around in the time I had been given, not only would BA terminate Concorde's operation, but so too would Air France, who were bleeding money even more profusely. As his message sunk in, it dawned on me that the immediate future of supersonic civil aviation rested on this turnaround and, with no time to waste, I clearly needed support if I were to stand any chance of success. Though not a flight per se, my immediate response was to revert to my flying habit prayer and ask God for help. More apt than I knew at the time, it would be a miracle if we were to succeed

in shifting the tide at Concorde, as my summons to Lord King's office and the formation of the Concorde division in May 1982 was much more than a response to my letters. It was also the culmination of a major internal reorganisation at BA which had begun a few years prior under the chairmanship of Sir Ross Stainton. Up to that point, since her first supersonic passenger flight in 1976, Concorde had been getting very little management support and was considered to be the lame duck of the BA fleet. With a palpable sense that Concorde was being set up to fail, an outcome no one wanted to be tarnished with, I might well be the scapegoat. Having stuck my head above the parapet with my multitude of letters, I had got what I asked for, and so had they. With an optimistic pilot now at the helm, the Board could wash their hands of the problem and watch her demise from a safe distance.

From an objective perspective, they had a case. Concorde was losing £16 million a year, a very considerable sum at that time, which was greater than the profitability of the entire airline. To add to the financial pressure she was experiencing, shortly after the formation of the division the £20 million annual support costs that the Government had been funding were pushed back on to BA, and subsequently on to the Concorde division itself. With such a vast scale of losses there was a mountain to climb to reach profitability and my immediate priority to join me in this mission came in the form of First Officer (later Captain) Jock Lowe. Jock was always my first choice, and his acceptance of my offer commenced what was to become a very effective collaboration.

As a co-pilot and instructor, with a reputation for being a bright spark, Jock was a no brainer for me, and thankfully he felt the same and did not hesitate to join me. We shared a tiny office and worked well as a unit in a friendly and effective manner, with each of us taking on different tasks, undergirded by an unwavering trust in each other. A flight deck is to a large extent a controlled environment, with numerous predetermined and sophisticated checklists to follow. To suddenly find ourselves in a commercial world, with no guidance or routine, was a bit of a shock for both of us, but we discussed problems head on, often laughing at the things we learnt, and I do not ever remember a disagreement between the two of us. Driven by the huge challenge ahead, initially we had virtually no knowledge of the processes of the commercial department we were building, but Jock's reputation proved to be more than true and with our seatbelts securely fastened, we were to enjoy many "Concorde firsts" together over the years.

At the same time as the BA shake-up, I was also juggling my faith exploration, reading when I could at home and between flights whilst travelling. It was on one such trip to New York that I finally felt as though I had "met God", on paper at least; the lightbulb had gone on. Prior to my thorough research, I did not feel any need of God. If someone had asked me if I needed God, I think I would have raised my eyebrows and reminded them of all I had achieved, being at the top of my profession, with all the blessings a man could want, and that I had done it all myself. After all my studying and research, I began to understand that everything I had, had been given to me *by*

God: my ability to fly aeroplanes, my wife, my children, the opportunities I had been encouraged to take and my career path – everything had come from God and I found myself actually enjoying unravelling the fullness and new life of that mystery whilst, at the same time, endeavouring to change the fortunes of an airline division heavily in the red!

The day after Lord King set me the challenge, new life also appeared at Concorde as the shackles came tumbling down. Many of the elements that had been restricting progress, inhibiting change and causing me to write letters, could now be addressed head on. Thankfully, Concorde herself was not the problem, so there was no need to modify the aircraft, only the way in which she was being operated, managed, marketed and ultimately the way in which the promised service was actually delivered to our customers. Concorde passengers were buying more than a ticket to a destination; they were buying excellence, status, a dream. But up until that point, what they received was a far cry from those ideals. They were high flyers in their lives, certainly high flyers on our aeroplane, and they were accustomed to the "golden age" style of travel, with everything being done to the highest of standards. Every area of our operation had to understand and represent this. No longer could we accept the excuses, such as why the plane was late being presented for loading passengers; or why there was never an acceptable response from catering when passengers had concerns about the food; or when all too frequently the stewards complained as they ran out of one product or another. Up until that point, Concorde had not been a priority for BA and had regularly had to wait in line, depending on external factors over which we had no control. Consequently, we had no choice but to pass the delays and sub-par service on to our passengers. Finally, that could all now change. We could now set our own standards. As an airline within an airline, we had access to the entire BA back office and yet retained autonomy over our major decisions. The independent Concorde division for which we now had full accountability and responsibility enabled us to do things differently, to do them our way, and we could not wait to get started with the planned improvements.

Management of our dedicated Concorde division profit and loss also gave greater transparency to our financial situation and the scale of the commercial challenge we faced, bringing into sharp focus what we needed to achieve and the areas which required primary attention. With the financial analysis complete, Jock and I devised a three-point plan built around cost cutting, revenue growth and, most crucially, changing the perception of Concorde as the lame duck of the BA fleet. Cost cutting was a fairly simple exercise. Staff were accounting for a disproportionate percentage of our central overheads, so each department was tasked with tightening their belts and finding efficiencies which ultimately led, inter alia, to reducing our flight crews and changing (for the good) the working arrangements of the cabin crew and maintenance team.

Revenue growth had many facets, which Jock hit head on. For starters, through BA marketing team surveys Jock established, to our great delight, that the vast majority of business travellers assumed Concorde fares were far higher than they actually were. An open door through which we didn't need a second invitation, this enabled us to bring the fares more in line with actual cost and value, without any impact on demand. Working closely with BA's commercial team, we also explored new routes, evaluating every potential viable market from Toronto and Boston to Lagos and Jeddah. Each additional route needed to satisfy stringent technical, commercial and operational considerations, and all paths led back to NYC and Washington as the high-value, high-demand ones we needed to plough our efforts into. Dulles International Airport in Washington DC was key, as it provided swift entry and exit to the US for government officials, and had been the first to give Concorde access to their runways. Other routes had been tried but lacked viability. We also explored partnerships, affiliating with Singapore Airlines and Dallas-based Braniff Airlines, and still another with Cunard to create a package for transatlantic cruise passengers to return on Concorde.

The final strand of our revenue growth strategy was the charters. When we started the division, though he chose not to join the team, my predecessor Brian Calvert offered many valuable suggestions, and was instrumental in encouraging us to expand Concorde operations using charter flights. He was spot on with his judgement. Making Concorde available for charter, an initiative enabled through the invaluable support of BA's own head of charters, George Blundell-Pound, was a hugely beneficial development for our division. The charters brought new destinations into play such as Barbados, Singapore, Cyprus,

Egypt, Australia, New Zealand and even Lapland, and also included a three-week round-the-world charter as well as round-robin flights over the Channel Islands, the North Sea and the Bay of Biscay. All of a sudden, people who dreamt of flying faster than the speed of sound rather than arriving at their destination sooner, could experience those dreams being realised. Though financially the charters contributed no more than ten per cent of our overall revenues, they delivered so much more reputationally through the publicity they generated, together with the huge impact that they had on operations as their increase on demand helped to maintain all seven aircraft in a serviceable state.

Whilst Jock spearheaded our pricing strategy for revenue growth, I was more focused on our marketing, the newly introduced charter flights fast becoming a significant part of that strategy and at no cost to us. Given the travel companies selling the charters were also footing the marketing bill, it was a win-win for our division. Beyond this, I embarked on a series of promotional speaking engagements, travelling extensively to speak with many of the major corporations who made up our core target market. The media onslaught I had experienced in New York had prepared me well and thankfully a more positive narrative was now beginning to emerge. I recall one time in 1983 travelling through South America down to its southernmost tip. Meeting with travel agents and marketing executives, I promoted the opportunity for their clients to get to Europe faster by linking up with the regular Miami to London Concorde service, which ran for many years. Other publicity initiatives included flying over numerous major sporting events; attending international air shows; flying in formation with the Red Arrows; and years later the flight of a four Concorde formation to celebrate the tenth anniversary of the inaugural Concorde flight; each in turn garnering extensive global media attention and creating iconic photographic memories.

BA's senior management became highly supportive in their attitude, and so left us to get on with the myriad of events we were running, and consequently our only accountability requirement for such events was simply to secure Civil Aviation Authority approval. All of our initiatives and the extensive media coverage we were generating, attested to the benefits of the operational autonomy we were now enjoying. As successful as we were, both Jock and I knew that if all the changes we had made were to sustain profitability, our enthusiasm alone was not sufficient. Concorde was a big step forward for aviation and I was very proud to be involved in trying to prove she was commercially viable and could be accepted as part of BA's future fleet. I knew how much brilliant work had gone into producing Concorde and if I could not prove its worthiness in operating it, then I felt I would have let down those who had contributed months and years to the design and development of it.

As a revolutionary aeroplane, Concorde did not just need her own staff, she needed a team as motivated as we were, who shared our passion and the same sense of ownership in her success. The dynamic had to shift and so, with renewed focus, we started communicating more regularly with managers across all areas of our business, from operations and engineering to catering and marketing. In many cases, we not only changed how we communicated but also improved the message we were conveying. In addition, we even adapted the timing of how messages were delivered, establishing a new way of working which boosted morale across the division. Often going the extra mile, this happened in different ways, such as the late-night visits I made to the hangar for chats with the ground engineers and the maintenance manager.

Previously, Concorde did not have her own dedicated maintenance hangar team, but rather shared them with other aircraft. Now that we were independent and Concorde specific, I could address the engineers responsible for Concorde directly. Sharing with them how our passenger numbers were growing and that their work preparing the aircraft had positively driven commercial benefits for the whole division, seemed to have the desired effect and attitudes began to change. The enhanced diligence in their respective roles became evident and it didn't stop there. Given our autonomous freedom, I was able to offer staff use of empty seats on our scheduled flights, the impact of this more than evidenced by their wide eyes as they shared in the luxury and elite company that a Concorde flight bestowed on her passengers.

Suited and booted, cleanly shaven, dressed to impress and belts firmly fastened, it proved an inspirational morale booster; not only were they taking off, so too were the attitudes across the division. The team took greater pride in their work, understood its positive impact, became more committed and – along with the many others across all areas who were key to delivering the Concorde experience – became integral to the turnaround we were starting to deliver. The tide was turning, and no longer were we operating at arm's length. Each person in their different function was embracing the vital role that was theirs to play, with a clear identity and a growing sense of unity, pride and purpose. At the end of the day, there was no silver bullet to turn around Concorde's fortunes. While it was far from the case that everything we touched turned to gold, I am proud to say that the majority of the new initiatives bore dividends through the hard work of every member of the Concorde division, alongside my own multitude of requests to God for *"help today"*!

Not only were the changes working in terms of attitudes, within just twelve months of the formation of the division, Concorde was starting to operate in profit. Lord King, a numbers man who had given me the two-year deadline, was closely monitoring our progress and he didn't shy away from letting this be known. I had always found him an easy man to speak with; he had no issues acknowledging achievements and praising when credit was due, a trait I respected. His approval meant so much more given his well-known intolerance of anything he considered detrimental to success and his renowned fortitude in following through on what he felt needed to be done, even if it was unpopular among the ranks. So it was, on more than one occasion, we found ourselves aboard the same aircraft, and he would offer the brief yet impacting encouragement of *"You're nearly there, Brian."* There was no room for sentimentality. I knew what he meant: that

I and the Concorde team had earned his respect, and I appreciated his willingness to say so.

After the successful first year, our growth continued apace and after three years we had turned the £16m annual loss into £50m annual profit, even while taking on all of the £20 million in support costs previously underwritten by the Government. As Concorde's commercial success improved, her in-house popularity soared. No longer were we the pariahs from whom senior BA executives shunned association. The *"commercial corpse"* was very much alive, and Concorde became part of the BA culture, with the airline enjoying her "halo effect" – Concorde's photogenic beauty and growing profile and success working commercial wonders on BA passengers who largely would never be able to settle into one of her prized seats.

One instance came in 1985 as we were approaching the tenth anniversary of Concorde's first commercial flight, which had taken place on 21st January 1976. A notable occasion worthy of celebrating, I met with a strategic few, including Jock Lowe and Adrian Meredith, to discuss how best to mark the occasion photographically. Whilst the thought of capturing all seven Concordes flying together was top of the list, this was not going to be possible as at least one or two were flying daily to New York. There was not, however, a lot of commercial activity for Concorde in the run up to Christmas, so we locked in on the idea that four Concordes fly in formation over the south of England as a commemorative flight. With a nod from the Chief Exec, it was all systems go for a flight, which though initially set for November, was eventually moved to Christmas Eve due to weather and availability. The captain, first officer and engineering officer for each aircraft were chosen from the senior Concorde crews, but not so the passengers. For all the interest in Concorde and the money which could have been made selling out all the seats for the celebratory hour-long flights, BA had another plan. Wanting to share the experience with as many of the Concorde family as possible, we decided that sixty-five seats on each aircraft would be given to BA staff and crews . . . , so that they could experience flying Concorde as a passenger.

With many hours of formation flying experience from my RAF days, I appreciated the opportunity to do so in the beautiful bird and was captain of plane 1, the lead plane. Understandably, a fair amount of logistics was involved in a formation flight of four Concordes and, needless to say, Jock was once again on hand to help. We were joined by a number of the other senior crew and, of course, BA's photographer Adrian Meredith. Having joined BA in 1976, Adrian had taken some of their most iconic photographs, and we were hoping for the same for the tenth anniversary formation flight, which he would be photographing from a Learjet in the skies with us. On the morning of the flight, I briefed the captains on the formation that we were to fly, including *diamond*, *swan like* and then *four-line abreast,* the *echelon*. With the Concordes timed to take off in quick succession from Heathrow, the Learjet with Adrian on board took off shortly before us and began circling as it waited for us to appear above the cloud cover. What happened next was, according to Adrian, quite amazing. Whilst circling in the jet, he saw the four Concordes each suddenly appear, literally popping out from the clouds like bullets, first one, then another, then the third and finally the fourth. Wasting no time, we quickly assembled at 15,000 feet and the Learjet with Adrian on board reduced height and caught up with us – obviously we were not flying supersonic!

Flying subsonic we made our way down over the south coast to Lands' End, moving from one formation to the other. Starting with the diamond formation, we then broke off through cloud before reassembling the aircraft together for the swan formation. We finished with the echelon, four abreast with our wing tips barely seventy feet apart, and thus produced one of the most iconic Concorde photographs ever to be taken, which fittingly adorns the cover of this book. While the plan had been to fly over the BA factory at Filton for colleagues there to see us, due to the cloud cover they only heard Concorde's familiar roar as we sped back to Heathrow under ATC's direction.

Given the cost of having four Concordes airborne for an hour and a half, it was quite likely the most expensive photo shoot to date for BA. I had worked with Adrian Meredith before and had always admired his work and found it first class. A very professional and efficient man, I had every confidence in him, but still remarked that after the vast expense of the shoot, I hoped the pictures came out well! Unfortunately for him, he had an agonising wait, for in those days we did not have instant development and it took a week for his film to be processed. Needless to say, they were well worth the wait, ensuring the legacy of the unique experience was captured for all to see. The picture went viral and was a PR gift, with the flight making headlines across the press. It also produced one of the photographs I have autographed the most over the years.

BA marketing executives clamoured for her images, increasingly keen to intertwine the two brands, and Concorde's profile would in time be considered every bit as valuable as her financial profitability. I am proud to say that in spite of all the challenges and sceptics, we brought a surprising smile to Lord King's face as we met and surpassed his target, and the rest, as they say, is history. Concorde's trajectory had shifted and was now very much a feather in the cap of BA. The perception and reality of the bird had changed, shifting from the *Lame Duck* to the *Golden Eagle* of the BA fleet; a turnaround achieved against every expectation of Lord King, BA senior management and a multitude of industry naysayers by the newly formed dedicated Concorde family. Concorde was finally free to soar.

8

The Passengers

Without passengers, airlines tend to grind to a halt. For every commercial airline, passengers are the lifeblood of the business and this was no different for Concorde. It was they who would define our success or failure. They who would keep us in flight. Everything we did was geared to the passenger experience; from the second they booked their sought-after seat to the moment we bid them *au revoir* as they disembarked from our ramp. Thankfully, the feeling was mutual. As much as we valued our passengers, they valued Concorde too. For our business passengers we provided "time-travel", delivering them in NYC "before" they left London, a full day of deal-making ahead of them. Sir David Frost once commented it was the only way in life you could "be in two places at once", the time-saving far outweighing the ticket costs. Invariably esteemed luminaries in their respective fields, the Concorde passengers were nonetheless enchanted by their Concorde affiliation.

As members of the exclusive club, our passengers expected the very best from start to finish. Even more so the celebrities and dignitaries, who though well versed in elite five-star service, still revered the Concorde experience and all that came with it. During the flight, the single-class passenger experience was primarily defined by exquisite service for our high-flying customers. Champagne, cocktails, caviar and lobster were integral to the menu and offered to all. There was no First, Business or Economy class, the streamlined body resulting in more of an office chair than armchair experience. Though in stark contrast to the first-class comfort on BA's 747s, it was a small price to pay for flying supersonic, and deemed even more acceptable when flight at 60,000 feet exposed the plane to less turbulence than experienced at the cruising altitudes of 747s and 707s, resulting in more champagne remaining in the flute! Meanwhile, our charter passengers were living their dreams, honorary members of that same exclusive club for an hour or more of their lives. They were flying at Mach 2, not to save time but because their lives coincided with the advent of supersonic commercial travel and they had the once-in-a-lifetime opportunity to enjoy her luxury whilst also becoming part of history.

Once flying at Mach 2, the captain's radio communication with the passengers was less frequent than on the 707, due to the shortened flight time and consequent greater intensity on the flight deck. Even so, once boarded and seated, I would always say a few words, often greeting them with, *"Welcome to Concorde, BA's unique supersonic operation. Today from London Heathrow to New York's John F. Kennedy our flight time will be three hours twenty-three minutes, which compares with the seven hours forty-five minutes of the subsonic alternatives,"* never missing the opportunity to affirm their choice of flying on Concorde. Mid-flight comments were equally loaded, with my regular preference being, *"Just to let you know how the flight is progressing – the answer is quickly!"* My comment of choice for north Atlantic flights was a variation of *"If you look out to our starboard side, you will see a Pan American aircraft also en-route to New York, looking as though it is going backwards."* It never failed to amuse and no doubt was recounted at many a dinner table over the years, as was the stunning experience of seeing the curvature of the earth, which I would point out on particularly clear days. My final sign-off after landing, our workload complete, was less humorous and a little more reflective than the others: *"We trust that your experience was one you'll forever appreciate, and wish you well on your onward journey,"* hopeful but never presuming that the passengers appreciated their Concorde experience as much as I did.

Unlike long-haul flights in a 707 or similar, when the captain could rest his eyes for a few minutes, catch up on notes, or even enjoy the luxury of reading a newspaper or magazine, on Concorde there was none of that. All too mindful of the many checklists we had to go through at a far more rapid pace than on other aircraft, flying Concorde demanded your full attention. Reflecting these demands on the flight deck, during flight my announcements were usually brief, but we never lost sight of the value of interacting with our passengers and took advantage of the opportunities we had to ensure their journey was an experience they appreciated.

Prior to departure, a load sheet detailing the number of passengers on board, specific valuable cargo being transported and any important considerations, would need to be signed by the captain, and so would be brought to the flight deck by a British Airways executive for signature, once the passengers and cargo were safely on board. While delivering the load sheet, if dignitaries were travelling with us the executive would usually then share that, *"By the way, you've got so and so in seat 26C . . ."* although, to be fair, we usually already knew this from the chief steward! Once airborne and cruising at Mach 2, I would often suggest to the steward that they might like to offer a few selected VIPs the opportunity to see the flight deck, insisting always that it be made clear the visit would be brief. It was an invitation which was seldom declined, regardless of the passenger's status or frequency of flight.

Unlike other aircraft, Concorde crews and their passengers were a small and tight-knit community, and all equally valued members of the overall Concorde family. No matter who you were (unless of course you were a member of our Royal Family) for just over three hours (and on rare occasions slightly under!) you had parity with the other ninety-nine passengers, many of whom hailed from the rich and famous of their time. British royalty; presidents, prime ministers and other political leaders; sporting elites from Muhammed Ali and David Beckham to Arnold Palmer and Bjorn Borg; rock stars from Sir Mick Jagger and The Beatles to Sir Elton John; Hollywood royalty from Elizabeth Taylor and Robert Redford to Dame Joan Collins and Liza Minelli; Nobel Prize winners, senior corporate executives, professionals and ultra-high-net-worth individuals – they all stepped aboard and joined the Concorde family.

Equally, but no less importantly, we welcomed those who parted with their life savings for a once-in-a-lifetime experience. Though Concorde's scheduled services attracted the powerful, rich and famous, it was our charter flights which made the aircraft much more openly accessible. Given the taxpayers' support of the project in its early days, without which there would never have been a BA Concorde, it was both right and deeply satisfying to make the dream of supersonic flight a reality for the wider public, such as the popular standard charter flight which went out over the west coast of England, taking in the Channel Islands. About an hour of total flying time, subsonic and supersonic, these flights had an additional pilot on board, seated in the jump seat, specifically positioned to give commentary to the passengers throughout the journey, pointing out each of the Channel Islands and other points of interest as we flew. The passengers were also brought up to the flight deck in fifty pairs, so it was a brief visit, but still served to satisfy the desire for the Concorde experience, which for many peaked as we inched ever closer to that all important 1,350mph. Though not there to witness it myself, the cabin staff often mentioned the excitement in the cabin being most visible as we reached supersonic, beaming facial expressions revealing just how much the experience meant. Whilst many of our well-known regulars got used to the Concorde experience, she still had the ability to induce a degree of humility in the many high-flying passengers, who in other aspects of life were arguably not blessed with accepted norms of self-doubt. Most were in awe of the miracle of engineering by which they had supersonically crossed the Atlantic, resembling excited children as they pointed at every dial when invited up to the flight deck. Their overly expressive gratitude to the crew on disembarking never got old and spoke of the enchanting aura that Concorde possessed.

In 1971, when just thirty-seven years old, not long after I was promoted to Captain, I was given the great honour of flying Her Majesty Queen Elizabeth II aboard a BA 707 from Honolulu to Guam, Hong Kong, Tokyo, Anchorage and finally on to London, with each stop lasting for three or four days. When asked if I ever felt nervous about such a responsibility, I would explain that my philosophy has always been that if I'm up the front and I arrive safely, the back will follow perfectly securely! Spending time with the Queen over the course of that trip, I became increasingly impressed by her intelligence, alertness, distinct lack of self-importance and wholly engaging personality as she absorbed the flight charts and inquired endlessly about speed, distance, altitude and location. Having enjoyed this privilege in the earlier part of my career, to fly her again aboard Concorde was doubly rewarding. The occasion came at the end of the Queen's Silver Jubilee year in 1977, when we were asked by Buckingham Palace if we could meet the Queen in Barbados, where she was travelling on the Royal Yacht *Britannia* as part of her Jubilee tour, and return her to London. We were delighted with the request but needed to overcome a few complexities before we could accept, not least a fuel issue.

Barbados airport at the time had a very short runway, (impacting the take-off weight) so we needed to check we could load enough fuel in Barbados for the non-stop flight home. After running computer models and tail wind forecasts for nearly three weeks, we confirmed with the Palace that it was viable and agreed to the flight, and excitement mounted among the crew as the honour of flying our sovereign drew ever closer. During our flight out to Barbados, a member of her senior staff suggested we ourselves might like to bestow an honour on Her Majesty. To announce our arrival and let the Queen know Concorde was there to take her home, he suggested we pay tribute to her with a low-level fly past as we arrived in Barbados. The senior staff member had the radio frequencies of the Royal Yacht *Britannia*, and suggested I use them to radio and ask for the latitude and longitude of their location. Though already busy with the usual landing procedures, I duly obliged and the wheels were in motion for our slight detour.

Decelerating as we started our descent, and with the search radar on, we soon located a little spec close to Antigua and Barbados, which we determined was the Royal Yacht *Britannia*. Sure enough, as we descended, there before us was the Royal Yacht, the billowing Royal Standard indicating the Queen was on board, and the fly past commenced. For maximum effect, we flew quite low and close to the ocean as we circled the Royal Yacht, and banking left were greeted by Her Majesty the Queen and the Duke of Edinburgh waving enthusiastically to us from the aft deck of *Britannia*. Flying a full circuit of the Royal Yacht, we circled back and continued on to Grantley Adams International Airport and disembarked. After enjoying a small rum and coke, believing the event had been a roaring success, I retired to my hotel room, ready for a good night's sleep.

The following morning, it did not take long for the bigger picture to unfold. I had not long been awake when my bedside phone rang and the hotel operator politely informed me that the BA Director of Flight Operations was on the line, wanting to speak with me. Given the nature of our trip, I assumed a call from the senior office was a courtesy call and happily waited for him to be transferred. It came, therefore, as somewhat of surprise when he barely said good morning before rather anxiously informing me that the front of the *Daily Telegraph* had a full-page picture of me flying Concorde round the Royal Yacht *Britannia* with the Queen and Duke of Edinburgh clearly seen giving us an animated reception. My initial response was delight at such unexpected publicity for Concorde, but his tone suggested I was missing the point.

The occasion had been seen by vast swathes of the public, with the Queen's obvious delight at the fly past being heralded across the front pages of the national press and further afield. The only glitch in this PR gift for Concorde was that the British public were not the only ones who saw the photographs which captured, in the opinion of the Civil Aviation Authority (CAA), an unacceptably low fly past. The BA Operations Director further informed me that the CAA were requesting an explanation as to why Concorde was flying so close to the ocean and the Royal Yacht, and precise data on the exact distances. With a working hypothesis that low-flying regulations had clearly been violated, the CAA were also threatening to prohibit the return flight for the Queen, pending receipt of the full facts.

Knowing who I thought should resolve this mess, before seeking data and evidence from my crew I made a bee-line for the staff member who had suggested the fly past! I explained to him in no uncertain terms the embarrassment the event had caused for both British Airways, Concorde and myself, and reminded him whose idea the fly past was in the first place. Finally, I explained that without CAA approval, the return flight would not be permitted to proceed. Needless to say, it wasn't long after this conversation that a statement was issued on behalf of the Queen *"congratulating Captain Walpole on an excellent display of low-level flying"* and inviting any questions relating to the aforementioned fly past to be addressed directly to the Palace. To our relief, that was the end of the matter and the return flight proceeded without delay, with the Duke of Edinburgh enjoying time in the flight deck, eager to see for himself the workings of supersonic flight.

Though this was the only time I had the honour of flying her on board Concorde, Queen Elizabeth II and other members of her family were regular passengers. It may surprise some, however, that many of the most pertinent questions I was asked about the specifics of Concorde came from their matriarch, the late Queen Elizabeth the Queen Mother. As was to be expected, she did not experience the same time strictures on the flight deck as other passengers, and I recall a most delightful interlude for her birthday in August 1985. Having been informed that she had not experienced Concorde in flight, Lord King had specifically requested, in recognition of her eighty-fifth birthday, that I fly her around the United Kingdom on a special celebratory flight. Whilst she would obviously be assigned seat 1A, as usual on such flights, we needed people in the back seats to balance the flight. For ease of decision, we came up with a simple way of selecting BA staff to enjoy the event – those staff who had a birthday nearest to the Queen Mother's! With the back of the aircraft filled with excited BA staff from across a myriad of departments, be they catering, engineers, marketing or otherwise, it did not take long for some to realise a friend from their department was on board, and so began the seat swapping. Before the Queen Mother's arrival, her equerry came onboard to check all was in order and, to his horror, noticed people were not in their assigned seats. Without hesitation, he quickly explained that she had been briefed on the people who would be on the flight based on their seat location and explained, therefore, that they all needed to quickly return to their original seat.

With Her Majesty on board, accompanied by two of her grandchildren, we set off flying north subsonic, near to her home in Castle of Mey. Whilst in flight, the Queen Mother did indeed venture down towards the back of the aircraft, and I am sure the joy for some when she spoke to them and knew their names and jobs, more than made up for not sitting next to a friend. One such passenger was Adrian Meredith, of course not selected for his birthday but rather for his capturing of her historic trip. Approaching Adrian, she asked if flying supersonic affected the camera and he explained that it did not. Thankfully for us, he was correct and again captured a wonderful image of her receiving a birthday cake on board and also happily ensconced in the jump seat later in the flight. Having reached the east coast of Scotland, banking right, we accelerated to Mach 2 coming down the North Sea, and then decelerated to subsonic as we came across the built-up area on the outskirts of London, heading to Heathrow. I remember saying to her as we turned in for a final approach to the runway, *"There's a place you might recognise, Your Majesty, down there."* As we banked to turn west, she delightfully responded, *"Oh yes, it's Buck House,"* obviously known more commonly to the rest of us as Buckingham Palace!

Another notable female leader of this era was Margaret Thatcher. During her tenure as Prime Minister of the United Kingdom, I had flown Margaret Thatcher half way round the world in a BA 707, but never had she travelled on Concorde. That was all to change when my wife Rosemary and I were rather surprisingly invited to a dinner at 10 Downing Street. No. 10 was not a dinner location we frequented, but on this occasion my attendance was required due to a formal visit from the Indian Prime Minister, Rajiv Gandhi. Prior to his political life, Mr Gandhi had been a pilot with Indian Airlines, a detail which caused the brainstorming minds in Downing Street to surmise the former aviator might wish to discuss Concorde. With this anticipated narrative surpassing the knowledge base of the current invitation list, my attendance was deemed a rather urgent necessity. They needed my help with his anticipated questions and, unbeknownst to them at the time, I needed the PM's help with my own question. Invitation duly accepted, Rosemary and I attended, and though contrary to all projections, no conversations of real Concorde significance with Mr Gandhi ensued. The evening did, however, prove to be of huge significance for Concorde.

With dinner concluded, all the guests made their way up the grand cantilevered stairs of No. 10, adorned with portraits of all the prime ministers of yesteryear, to the after-dinner reception where Mrs Thatcher and her husband Dennis began making their way through the assembled company. Seizing the moment, as the Prime Minister came within striking distance, I took the opportunity to approach her with my question. "*Yes, Captain Walpole, what can I do for you?*" The answer was simple yet extremely significant – would she endorse Concorde by flying on her, something she had hitherto never done?

Mrs Thatcher was not backward in her response, nor did I expect her to be. Afterall, she was known as the Iron Lady for a reason. To her, the answer was twofold: "*Number one, I would be concerned about the level of security, Captain Walpole. Number two, it would be seen to be profligate for the Government to charter Concorde at the prices you elect to charge.*" Knowing this was likely to be my only opportunity to pursue this cause, my response needed to impress. Thankfully with the autonomy we were now enjoying at Concorde, I was in a position to negotiate. *"Prime Minister,"* I replied, *"on your first point, I can assure you our security measures will meet the standards appropriate for you and your team. On your second, I'm happy to offer the aeroplane to you and your office for charter, at cost."* It seemed my response was noted, and looking me firmly in the eyes she informed me that she would bear my offer in mind, then continued on her way. Only time would tell whether or not my question would make a difference, but much to my delight we didn't have long to wait. About a month later we received a call from Downing Street requesting Concorde to fly Margaret Thatcher to Vancouver in July to open the British Pavilion for Expo 86. My audacious gamble having paid off, the answer was of course a resounding, *"With pleasure,"* and the requisite planning commenced immediately.

Concorde's noise compliance policy, which I knew very well, stipulated that we always stuck rigidly to the rule of not flying supersonic over populated areas due to the sonic boom. The noise from the boom had come onto my radar relatively early in my Concorde life, when I had heard talk of the surprise it caused. Knowing that if I was to speak with any authority on the matter I needed to experience it for myself, I travelled to various locations where I knew I could witness an overflight of Concorde flying supersonic. Experiencing first-hand the fright of the boom carpet coming towards you, it was startling – the reports were by no means exaggerated. Needless to say, I returned convinced it was unacceptable to fly supersonic over inhabited land, and affirmed our noise policy! With that in mind, as part of the pre-flight preparation I asked Downing Street to secure permission from the Canadian authorities for a supersonic overflight of the vast expanse of Canada, to ensure the maximum benefits of supersonic speed for the Prime Minister on her weekend trip. Permission granted, we took off from London Heathrow in the evening for Gander in Newfoundland, refuelled, then departed for Vancouver, climbing up at Mach 2 past Churchill, a town on Hudson Bay in the far north of Manitoba, Canada. It was at this stage of the flight that the Prime Minister came up on the flight deck and addressed me directly. *"Captain Walpole, I am so impressed by this aircraft, the leather seats, superb cuisine and look at this . . ."* I watched as she took a pound coin out of her much-vaunted handbag, placed it on the pedestal behind the throttles, stood it on its side and looked at me, astonished.

While I was somewhat less amazed, Mrs Thatcher was, quite simply, awe struck that the coin stayed on its side while travelling at twice the speed of sound. Delighted by the surprises she was enjoying on board, she then returned to her seat, only to reappear just as we were starting our descent. *"Captain Walpole, may I ask of you that when I open the UK Pavilion tomorrow, you could perform a fly past in Concorde, because I think it would impress the world."* Assuring her that I would be more than happy to fulfil her request, provided the plane was serviceable in that time, she again departed the flight deck, an even more contented demeanour across her face. I too was delighted – not only that the Prime Minister was seeing her first trip on Concorde in such a positive light, but also given the perfect opportunity I would once again have to do some low-level flying, something I hadn't "officially" done since my Air Force days, the Queen's fly past aside!

With servicing necessities fulfilled, the next day we flew across the multitude of Expo pavilions at an altitude of just 1,000 feet, a height at which I could very clearly make out the smiling face, waving hand and ever-present handbag of Margaret Thatcher. With crowds duly wowed and a successful visit under our belts, we later departed. Her praise and excitement on our return flight to England reassured me that this would not be the last time we saw Mrs Thatcher on Concorde, a sentiment she affirmed in a letter sent to me very shortly thereafter. Proclaiming it a magnificent journey, she noted that it had *"never occurred to me before to travel 12,000 miles for the weekend, and it certainly would not be possible by any other means,"* and further expressed her gratitude for the fly past which had *"attracted enormous interest and was a real triumph"*. Needless to say, Mrs Thatcher became one of our most powerful friends and allies in the years that followed.

A common feature on Concorde, passengers from the sporting world often generated a murmur of excitement among those crew members with a penchant for their specific sport of distinction. As a keen golfer, it was a particular delight in 1987 to welcome the European Ryder Cup team aboard as they headed to Muirfield Village, Ohio, in pursuit of a first Ryder Cup win on US soil. The now customary Concorde travel for the European team had started a few years prior, at the beginning of Tony Jacklin's leadership, when with only six months to go before the 1983 Ryder Cup, he had been asked to captain the side. As surprised as he was to receive the request, Tony had one condition – full autonomy (a concept we understood well at Concorde). Freedom granted, the very first thing he did was to demand they travelled on Concorde like the US team, which served as a huge morale boost for the European team. Sadly, Ryder Cup history shows they still lost, but only just! Two years later, once again under Tony's leadership, the tide turned and the Ryder Cup was returned to Europe in 1985.

Adamant that the morale-boosting Concorde travel needed to continue for the next iteration, with much creative planning the 1987 flight was confirmed. Funded by twenty to thirty wealthy fans, they delighted in parting with some of their sterling in exchange for VIP travel alongside the golfing superstars on the flight over. So it was, as the team boarded the flight on 21st September 1987, Tony Jacklin, the victorious captain from 1985, was at the helm again and approached me with a request. Considering the flight deck to be the safest place for the actual Cup itself, he wanted to leave it with us for the duration of the flight. For those not familiar with the Ryder Cup, as a hugely significant piece of sporting silverware (although actually made out of gold) it was a responsibility we enjoyed, and one which has triggered many a tinge of envy from golf-loving friends over the years. With the team all kitted out in matching uniform with crests on their chests, without doubt the greatest superstar amongst them was the phenomenal talent of the Spaniard Severiano Ballesteros, Seve as he was affectionately known by friends and strangers in equal measure.

As their talisman, Europe were relying on Seve, but when I went back into the cabin to greet the team I discovered he had a problem. With a terrible fear of flying, Seve was sitting there white knuckled, frozen in his seat and clearly in some discomfort. Having experienced many nervous passengers over the years, I suggested he might feel more comfortable in the jump seat on the flight deck. Quick to accept, he was soon buckled in and growing increasingly relaxed as the journey proceeded. Seve keenly credited his diminishing fear of flying to witnessing first-hand the operation of the plane – both the sophistication of the flight deck and also the calmness of our crew. Such was the turnaround in demeanour, that when Seve wasn't in the jump seat, nerves calmed, he was hitting a twenty-foot putt down the aisle of the cabin. At the time, this was the world's longest putt, travelling two to three miles in the time it took to roll down the plane. This was, however, one record Seve did not keep, being surpassed as he was in 1999 by his countryman Jose Maria Olazabal on his own way to the Ryder Cup, who managed to keep his ball in motion for long enough to cover over nine miles!

A decidedly eventful flight was rounded off in the only appropriate way, when I spotted Muirfield Village whilst circling at the Ohio airport and duly requested a fly past. Though initially refused, just as we were coming into land Air Traffic Control acquiesced and gave us the go ahead. Requiring a swift and rather loud ascent, we swept by

Muirfield and apparently gave some of the US team, who were out practising on the course, a rather unexpected surprise. Asked recently about that flight, Tony Jacklin still believes the use of Concorde was significant for the overall morale of the team. *"The team had a quiet confidence,"* he said. *"They felt like a team; had real pride and were being treated right."* Delighted to assist in calming the nerves of the incredible sporting genius that was Seve, pampering the European team and giving the US team a loud fly past, it might be a stretch to claim any credit for Seve's 2&1 win over Curtis Strange in the Sunday singles which sealed the European victory that year, but I like to think we most certainly played our part!

Whoever the passenger, whether royalty, sporting genius or lesser-known ticket holders, we were always respectful that they had put their trust and money in the service we were offering, but that still did not prevent our patience from being mildly tested at times. One such passenger was Graham Lacey himself, when he came to the cockpit to complain about my lack of communication whilst I was dealing with a double lightning strike. I was no stranger to being struck by lightning, having experienced it several times during my decades of flying. Whilst it sounds terrifying, as the training kicks in, it is more the shock that you have been hit that you have to deal with, rather than the effect it has on your flight. Once you realise you have been struck and then subsequently ascertain that everything is still working properly, you are just left with the shock of the strike, rather than a fear that you are in danger. Graham's recollection of the double strike given in the earlier "Preface" gives account of the incident, and though it was not his finest moment, he's more than redeemed himself since and we've enjoyed a subsequent laugh or two about it over the years.

Passengers would approach us on departure, eager to convey their appreciation, often leaving their business cards with an open invitation to assist anytime and anywhere, some of which proved rather useful at times when my son was seeking a summer job! Others had unique ways of expressing their gratitude, as on the occasion when we landed at Heathrow after experiencing exceptional tailwinds resulting in a flight time of just under three hours. With some pleasure I announced to the passengers that they had been part of one of the fastest ever crossings of the Atlantic, only to be met by a businessman who showed his face on the flight deck as he was disembarking, shook my hand, congratulated me on a superb flight but admitted to one disappointment. When I enquired what this was, anticipating that his champagne had been insufficiently chilled or his smoked salmon slices were not generous enough, he simply remarked that he had enjoyed the flight so much, he wished it could have lasted longer. Short of moving New York and London a little further away from each other, I expressed my regret that this would sadly not be possible, but I welcomed the sentiment.

Such was the uniqueness of the experience on Concorde, a number of our passengers wished to remember the occasion in a far less conventional way. One sports star, who shall remain nameless, would always invite a few uncomfortable looks each time he disembarked one of our flights. Unquestionably wealthy enough to be able to afford the finer things in life, Concorde offered something that money could not buy (at the time) – bespoke branded cutlery. The clanking of disappearing knives and forks from the depths of his many pockets raised the eyebrows of all those present, crew and passengers alike. Displaying the same self-confidence which had carried him to sporting greatness, the clanging clearly proved of no great embarrassment as he strode off the plane into the terminal, excited to relocate the cutlery to its new home. I took the view that he was not only a much-loved sporting hero but a good person, a regular passenger and that this was a small price to pay for his custom, and quietly encouraged the crew to adopt a blind eye or, more specifically, a deaf ear policy to his behaviour. To this day, I have often wondered how many sets he could muster around the dining room table for his guests to enjoy. Perhaps, if his family is reading this, they'd like to let me know!

Suffice it to say, wherever she went, people of all ages and stages, creed and colour, were fascinated by the magnificence of Concorde, and, at the end of the day, it was the same privilege and responsibility to fly all passengers from each and every walk of life. Commercially, we flew the most beautiful and powerful bird in the sky and it was an experience I wanted to share, and not just for commercial reasons. Concorde was one of those life experiences that served as a great leveller; the engineer in his free seat at the back, the once-in-a-lifetime charter passengers who had spent their life savings, the CEO and the pop star were all equal as passengers in my care. Whatever their reason for taking one of the seats in the finely manicured interior of Concorde, flying faster than any previous generation of commercial traveller, each and every one of our passengers became part of aviation history.

9

In-Flight Entertainment

Thankfully never seeming to diminish the passenger experience, it may surprise my grandchildren and their generation to learn that as the twentieth century was drawing to a close with Concorde leading the way in cutting-edge technology, the aircraft contained no in-house media entertainment at all. Though offering a plentiful supply of daily newspapers, no individual screens adorned the headrest of the seat before you; not even a main screen at the front of the cabin for the passengers to view a Hollywood classic as they sped across the skies. Small and seemingly unremarkable in appearance, there was, however, one very important "screen" in the cabin – the Mach Meter. Situated on the bulkhead, with its simple needle and dial, as its name might suggest, the Mach Meter monitored the speed, indicating when we were cruising at Mach 1 and then Mach 2. Needless to say, it attracted the keen attention of most of the passengers as they eagerly awaited our arrival at Mach 2, and it was important they looked, otherwise they could have missed the iconic moment.

When Concorde went supersonic, anyone on the ground below was all too aware due to the noise of the "boom carpet" which could be heard long before any sight of the aircraft. However, rather unexpectedly for many, unless the passengers onboard looked at the Mach Meter, or until we announced we had hit Mach 1 or 2, those onboard were oblivious to this and would have no idea they were travelling supersonic, such was the mastery of Concorde's design. There was no bang, no sudden thrust, no alarm bells, nothing of that ilk. After the initial thrust on take-off, the gentle noise of the engines roaring through the cabin as you were pushed back into your seat a little more forcefully than on other aircraft, there followed the deceptively smooth acceleration of the aircraft through to its cruising speed of 1,350mph. Therefore, as a passenger on Concorde, you were not aware of the noise below caused by the shockwaves created as the aeroplane flew faster than the speed of sound. Nor were the passengers aware that the aircraft even stretched in length by close to ten inches when flying supersonic, such were the friction and high temperatures generated on her frame at those speeds. The expandable fuselage and the specially designed paint used on Concorde allowed for the stretch and even dissipated the heat – further examples of the mind-boggling mastery of her design.

Speeding supersonically across the skies, the 100 passengers safely nestled into their office-like seats received exemplary service as they enjoyed their Concorde experience; a fact I can personally confirm, having had the pleasure of enjoying the Concorde experience from both ends of the plane! Though usually in the cockpit, there were occasions when I was heading to a meeting and thus enjoyed Concorde as a passenger. Usually seated in the back, in the "spare seats", as in any organisation, it was always interesting to observe things from the customer perspective. Though the crews usually knew who I was and subsequently afforded me an element of respect as someone senior in their organisation, their demeanour with all the passengers was first class in every respect. Not surprisingly, I was happy as a passenger and never minded being at the back of the plane rather than in the captain's seat as the Mach Meter reached that much vaunted 2.

One occasion when I was in the captain's seat cruising supersonic over the Atlantic on a rather eventful flight between Heathrow and JFK, there *were* external events which the passengers were all too aware of inside the aircraft. A couple of hours into the flight, I momentarily left the co-pilot at the flight deck and went to the bathroom, located immediately behind the flight deck. Just as I was returning, I heard the dreaded fire warning alarm on one of the engines. Quickly getting back in my captain's seat, I commenced the fire drill on number one engine, which included shutting the engine down. Before that occurred, we were at 60,000 feet travelling at 1,350mph. Reduced to three engines, I urgently sought clearance from Air Traffic Control (ATC), and immediately decelerated to subsonic. Descending rapidly to circa 38,000 feet we reduced our speed to a modest 600mph. Once stabilised and cruising, I spoke to the passengers and explained the need to shut down one of the engines, reassuring them that though

Concorde needed all four engines to fly supersonic, the aeroplane was perfectly well equipped to fly subsonically, and our journey would simply take a little longer.

As we approached JFK, an unforecast fog was rolling in. Thick fog is not a friend of air travel, and such was the height of this particular cloud cover that we were required to conduct an automatic landing as the cloud of fog was below the minimum height required for visibility to land manually. Though news of the fog was not a surprise to those in the window seats, I updated the passengers as we approached NYC. As our approach advanced, ATC advised that visibility had dropped even further and was now down close to 300m. When travelling at 170mph, on an automatic landing, these distances mean you are not going to see the lights until you get within just a couple of hundred feet of the runway!

Concorde had two automatic pilots and, per procedure, we lined them both up for an automatic landing and started our descent. We were at 1,000 feet, descending down the instrument landing system which indicated that the runway which we could not see was indeed ahead of us, when one of the two automatic pilots dropped out. In a split second we were travelling at 170mph, less than 1,000 feet from the runway, with one auto pilot instead of two and three engines instead of four. Preparing for what might happen next, and my heartfelt flight prayer silently uttered to the God I now felt I "knew", we sat poised to take the controls if needed, all too aware that if the second autopilot dropped out, we would have to perform a manual landing in very marginal conditions.

To the great relief of the entire flight deck, the autopilot stayed in, the automatic landing went smoothly and when we were just a couple of hundred feet above the ground, the runway came into view and we touched down safely. Full reverse on the three engines, instead of four, required increased breaking and we were all quite relieved as we came to a halt, as were the passengers who could be heard clapping enthusiastically in the cabin. It was a pleasing landing in marginal conditions, but we were certainly sitting quite close to the edge of our seats for that one.

In truth I was never scared in Concorde as I was always confident that I had enough knowledge and experience to deal with just about any problem. Such events were part of your training, and part of the job we chose to do. That said, the extended prayer I said many times in the course of my flying career, as I did that day, was, *"Lord God, please get us in safely and please ensure that I do the right things."* As my personal relationship with God grew, I became a great believer in asking Him for help. Even early on in my career when I was just saying it peripherally, not fully understanding who I was asking, I still felt it was worth it, but now my request had more authenticity.

Though the multi-screen construct of modern-day in-flight entertainment was nowhere to be seen on Concorde, over the years her flights still provided many amusing and extraordinary moments. Nearer the lower end of the risk continuum was my experience in 1986, at one of a number of appearances we made at the Toronto Air Show. Invited to undertake some low-level flying at 200 feet, we were always happy to share the wonders of Concorde's streamlined splendour, and on the conclusion of our display, once landed, I had the pleasure of being greeted on the flight deck by the Royal Canadian Mounted Police. Far from the usual tributes heralding the magnificence of the craft and the low-flying exhibition, to my surprise the Mounties proceeded to issue me with a charge sheet for the flight, which included speeding and jumping the traffic lights! Whilst briefly taken aback by the stern faces delivering the ticket, I very much appreciated their humour, taking it as a signal of their approval of Concorde and our flying that they went to the efforts of issuing a fake speeding ticket!

My refusal to pay the Mounties fine was, I believed, the most fitting response I could offer, which they in turn received with equal amusement. It also meant my speeding ticket record – across all forms of transport – remained clean, something I had worked hard to maintain in a previous, and equally bizarre encounter, a few years earlier in 1982 while in South Africa's Kruger National Park with my nineteen-year-old son. To my utter bewilderment, driving on a dirt track, scanning the bush for wildlife, far from anywhere and completely alone (or so I thought), I was clocked speeding by an officer. Upon returning to our rondavel, I disappeared to find the officer. Later, when my son enquired, *"How did it go, Dad?"* I somewhat proudly told him that the speeding ticket had been cancelled, and the officer was now the satisfied and rather excited owner of some well-travelled Concorde memorabilia. Impressed though he was, the fact that in the depths of one of the largest game reserves in the world I was delivered into the hands of a police officer with a passion for Concorde and her many exciting stories was not lost on me. Grateful for her global appeal, I was pleased to have escaped that punishment, and kept my licence clean.

As was to be expected when flying an aeroplane possessed with such engineering complexity, speed and power, Concorde provided its share of uncomfortably precarious moments as well. Highly trained as we were, at the end of the day there wasn't a manual for everything, a fact we were to experience first-hand during a flight out of Heathrow. Unlike on a car, the rigidity of aircraft tyres means that when depressurised they do not actually go flat. As such, the depressurisation of the tyre is not discernible to the naked eye. Whilst not visible, if one tyre lost pressure, the extra pressure loaded on its sister tyre would force it to explode when next employed on the ground.

On this particular flight, whilst taking off from London and for seemingly no apparent reason, a tyre had blown. With V1 passed, knowing the remaining length of the runway was insufficient for us to stop, we had no option at that point but to get airborne. As we took to the sky, the control tower came onto comms and advised we were streaming smoke out of our starboard undercarriage gear. With the scheduled flight and destination abandoned, the much-rehearsed emergency procedures kicked in and we quickly climbed to 20,000 feet in preparation for our return to London.

In order to land any aircraft, you have to get down to a maximum landing weight, which inevitably means you must not be carrying the majority of your fuel load. Per protocol, we went up the coast, and proceeded to dump over seventy-five per cent of our fuel; the fuel evaporating in the atmosphere as it descended. There is a limitation on how big the vents are for fuel release, so it's a relatively slow process and took about half an hour to unload, which gave me time to brief the passengers. On the radio, this time not with one of my amusing anecdotes, I reassured them that though we had a technical problem, we were perfectly safe, and explained that we would have to return to Heathrow. Confirming too that BA were preparing another Concorde to take them onwards to their destination, I left the cabin crew to brief the passengers for an emergency landing, reminding them of the brace position, and I began preparations to bring us down safely.

Fuel unloaded, we flew back to the airport and the tower suggested we come back round so that they could put their binoculars on us. Scanning the landing gear, they reported that the front pair of tyres (two tyres of four) on the starboard undercarriage were missing and informed us that they had never seen a Concorde land with tyres in that condition. With that less than comforting news received, we buckled down and prepared for what needed to be the smoothest landing we could possibly achieve, not knowing if the two remaining tyres would withstand the impact as we touched down on the tarmac.

Passengers suitably briefed, as we approached the runway, seat belts were tightened and no doubt a number of silent prayers echoed through the cabin as they braced for the unknown, fire engines and ambulances lining our pathway, their lights adding to the runway beacons anticipating our arrival. Mercifully we managed to grease the plane onto the runway, lifting the nose up higher than usual, causing the rear wheels to smoothly hit the ground, after which the nose gradually came down. As we came to a halt, there were no explosions or loss of control but the palpable relief of passengers and crew permeated the aircraft, as silence turned to murmurings of calm gratitude that we had landed safely back on terra firma. "*Well played,*" came the message from Air Traffic Control. "*Good landing.*"

The biggest reality check was the ambulances and fire engines lining the runway as we came in for the final approach, but thankfully despite never having been done before, it was all very measured in terms of braking and was quite a "good" landing. We landed safely; no-one was hurt and we did not even need to call for an emergency evacuation of the plane down the steps. During these what I named "unpleasant flights", of which there were a number over my career, there is no room for emotions. You have a job to do and you've been highly trained to do it and you get on with it. There was no fear mongering. There were no doom laden or despairing exchanges in the cockpit, of "*Oh, I hope this or that doesn't happen.*" My philosophy would kick in, knowing if I made it home safely, likely everyone would. With complete confidence in my co-pilot and flight engineer, our philosophy was to stay focused, go through our checklists, and be totally preoccupied with the requirements on the flight deck to get the plane safely on the ground. The reality is, as head of the Concorde division and Chief Captain of the Concorde fleet, I felt a great responsibility and regularly asked God for help; praying that I would make wise choices and not get it wrong, and regularly offering my gratitude for safe return home when unpleasant flights such as this occurred.

An investigation followed the incident and the assumption was that, given the freezing temperatures, the tyre had likely been penetrated by an ice spike. Further analysis was required, which somewhat bizarrely was to lead to one of the most unexpected and enthralling experiences in my Concorde career. Rather than relying on the eyesight and binoculars possessed by our control tower operators to check for tyre issues, a rather antiquated solution in the context of all that Concorde represented in terms of advanced technology, a new solution was presented by our engineers. It was determined that a torque meter fitted to the undercarriage would be our best solution. Torque is essentially force, so a torque meter would detect any change in force, which therefore meant that such a device could indicate on the flight deck if a tyre was flat – the force and formation of the tyre having changed if it was not at full pressure.

Given the need for French collaboration on any modifications to Concorde, I was required to cross the Channel to undertake tests with the Air France team to prove the veracity of this modification – namely that it showed a flat tyre and, of equal import, that it wouldn't give a false warning, which could likewise be calamitous. If the V1 for a flight, the point of no return I mentioned earlier, was at 160mph, a false warning at 150mph therefore would demand an immediate brake-burning stop – the heat generated on the brake pads likely destroying the undercarriage. As a result, flying with Air France's Captain Jean Franchi we had to perform what was called the "abuse case", which involved doing everything in our power to trigger a false warning by moving the rudder around aggressively during take-off. The basic requirement was to complete the procedure with fully pressurised tyres, and if there were no false warnings, this would indicate that the torque meter could be fully relied upon.

The torque meter test flight took place on a clear morning in 1986 on a pre-production Concorde with no passengers onboard, and just a technical crew surrounded by a mass of computers. With the French test pilot Jean Franchi and me on the flight deck, we had climbed up to 10,000 feet when, apropos of nothing, Jean turned to me and said, *"Brian, I'll show you that Concorde can do a complete barrel roll."* I quickly responded with my assumption he was pulling my leg, only to be met with his, *"No, we'll do it."* Jean was serious. We had excess fuel onboard and would need to fly around for fifteen minutes to use some of it to be weight compliant for landing, and he clearly thought this was a good way of expending the fuel more efficiently. Whilst noting this would not be his first time, he had, however, never performed one with anybody from the other side of the Channel on board, and so another "first" was on the horizon for this Englishman and Concorde.

Climbing to 15,000 feet, we advanced to 350 knots, positioned to 10° of pitch angle and then, before I knew it, we were accelerating into a 360-degree horizontal rotation as Jean Franchi performed the most graceful complete barrel roll to the left. Most people have no idea how their body will react to a sudden 360-degree roll, unsure whether their stomach will stay where it is or violently react to the change in gravity and the blood rushing to their feet – I had seen experienced aviators challenged by the experience. Having barrel rolled many times in the RAF, I knew what to expect and could enjoy my front-row seat, and the incredulous elation flowing through every fibre of my being as the manoeuvre unfolded before my very eyes. Suddenly, before I could even begin to contemplate what had just transpired, I was faced with another split-second decision – albeit less common than most I had faced in my lifetime – *"Brian,"* Jean said, *"I have been one way. I know you have a good pair of hands, now you'd better unwind it."* Taking me back to my RAF aerobatic adventures, I didn't hesitate. He'd rolled the plane left, and was inviting me to take it back the other way. I knew the key was to keep pulling positive-G all the way over (in other words, pull on the controls hard throughout the entire manoeuvre and accelerate fast) so that the roll completed. I took control, pulled away, and it worked beautifully, and around we went. Such was the mastery of the aircraft, some of the engineers down the back of the plane were unaware the manoeuvre had even happened due to the positive-G throughout. My manoeuvre was met with the relaxed nonchalance of Jean Franchi's, *"Nicely done, Brian,"* as we completed the roll, and whilst calm on the exterior, internally I was elated. It was a wholly unexpected experience; a quite astonishing school day like no other, and a gripping story which I have delighted in sharing with multitudes of listening ears in the years since.

Barrel rolls were the norm of air-to-air combat, when a navigator might call to a pilot to barrel roll starboard for example, causing the aircraft to lose speed so that the advancing enemy aircraft would fly past, leaving you poised with them in your sights. We were, however, not in a military aircraft and neither were we at war. Nonetheless, the confidence that the whole barrel roll experience in Concorde gave me, not that I needed any more in the aeroplane, was enormous; to know this magnificent ship could actually turn upside down and continue perfectly safely was next level. Nothing fell off, no red lights flashed, no instruments toppled. That to me was one of the most exciting things because it showed me what Concorde could do, and what an astonishing aeroplane she was: a civil aircraft, capable of doing not just one, but two barrel rolls in quick succession. To me, this solidified Concorde's status as the epitome of excellence in aviation.

Though an incredible experience, this was not the feasibility test we were airborne to check! With the torque meter modification tests dutifully completed on take-off, and our fuel load now duly reduced to requisite landing weight by the barrel rolls, our job was done and we returned to base. On my arrival in London, it did not take me long to share the barrel roll experience with Brian Trubshaw and, as I should have anticipated, he was distinctly unimpressed. As chief test pilot, he rather forcefully informed me that he had tested the aeroplane for years and that neither he, nor any one of his team, had ever performed a barrel roll, nor, for that matter, would they have deemed it appropriate to do so. Suitably reprimanded and humbled, I apologised, but nothing could diminish the even greater respect I then had for the brilliance of the engineering triumph of Concorde.

With the roll proudly noted in my log book, not surprisingly, word got out in the French media, and the story soon made its way across the Channel. Delighted to be associated with that aspect of Concorde's mastery, when asked about it as I often was, I was always keen to remind people that there were no passengers on board! Over time, I received a number of artists impressions trying to capture Concorde in full barrel roll. One in particular, which we've included in the book, seemed to depict the experience quite well, but no one-dimensional image can truly capture the flying marvel I experienced that day.

Equally surprising as the barrel roll in its suddenness and speed was my wife Rosemary's journey to faith in God. In contrast to her pedestrian aviator husband who spent years investigating and studying, Rosemary's journey did occur at supersonic speed! I was away on flying duty over a weekend and returned on the Monday to find Rosemary pale, nervous and somewhat pensive. Something had happened to her, but she wasn't quite over all the details. Rosemary had previously only joined me for one or two visits to Millmead church, so I was somewhat surprised to learn that she had visited during my absence. Recounting as best she could recall, she animatedly shared that she had woken up unusually early on the Sunday, feeling an unavoidable compulsion to go to church. Surprised by the overwhelming motivation, she had driven to Millmead on her own, arriving well before the service was even due to begin. Given her friendly demeanour, it surprised me that Rosemary made no mention of people she had met or spoken with, but I soon came to understand why. Her focus was the service and when it eventually began, Rosemary explained that she was riveted, listening to the words of the sermon, when, before she knew what was happening, she had an overwhelming feeling come over her whole body. Though it was not altogether clear to either of us exactly what she had experienced, Rosemary had nonetheless felt an intense sense of peace and lightness, both physically and mentally, as though a weight had been lifted off her. Unaware at the time what it was, we later came to understand she was experiencing the third part of the Trinity, the Holy Spirit, in what is often referred to as a Damascus Road experience, referencing the story of Saul in the Bible where he turned from his previous life and became a follower of Jesus.

As Rosemary nervously yet excitedly shared her experiences with me, with much detail still to be grasped, I realised that God speaks to us all differently and so magnificently uniquely. Rosemary and I are different people, and just like any parent, guardian, aunt, uncle, grandparent or godparent knows, each of the children we love so dearly are wired differently. God knows and understands this better than anyone. He knows we learn and process in different ways. He knows how our brains tick. He knows what is going to speak to each and every one of us, and Rosemary and I were no different: He knew what would work for each of us, and opened our eyes in two very unique ways, to the truth of who He is.

On my comparatively slow and research-laden journey, I came to realise that God was not some distant, abstract concept who observed from a distance. God knew everything about me, and loved me. Most of my life I did not understand how God and Jesus were connected, so one of the most satisfying discoveries was when I came to understand the fullness of their relationship. I discovered that not only was Jesus a man of history, but he was also God, who saved history; I discovered that the life and death of Jesus meant that I could have a different life, a life of hope both for now and for what was to come.

The more I understood, the more I realised that I, Brian Walpole, the egotist pilot, was simply a man who thought he had achieved everything in his own strength and abilities, but was finally coming face to face with the greater truth, seeing my life and the world in a whole new light. There grew in me an unabashed gratitude in knowing it is not good works nor achievements, but rather faith in Jesus Christ which is central to truly living: *"For it is by grace you have been saved, through faith – and this is not from yourselves, it is the gift of God – not by works, so that no one can boast"* (Ephesians 2:8-9). Whereas before I would look up to the sky with the eyes of a pilot and navigator, seeing particular stars and planets and thinking, *If I was navigating tonight, I'd be using this planet and that star.* Now things were different, and when I looked up, I saw the enormity and wonder of it all as God's creation. In acknowledging and appreciating, as never before, that

God is the ultimate creator of everything that I used to take for granted, I came to understand He gave it to us for our enjoyment, and entrusted His earth to our care. Far from how I may have once imagined Him as a distant creator, God was becoming the bedrock of my life and I started to chat to Him about everything, saying brief prayers (like my flight prayer) as I went about my day. I began asking Him for advice, help and strength with daily issues, seeking to know what He would have me do in any given situation.

As our faith grew, so did our desire to share it with our children. Perhaps the biggest difference in our family life was that Sunday was now the day for church. Conscious of not wanting to force our faith on our children, we encouraged them to come with us to church when they were home. Whilst we prayed for them privately, thanking God for the food before we ate at family meals and gifts of Bibles were further indications to them of our growing faith. Shelley, our youngest, was the only one living at home at that time, and recalls having numerous conversations with Rosemary about what exactly had happened to her in what Shelley describes as her mother's "radical conversion". Seeing her mother so incredibly excited about her faith and knowing who Rosemary was as a person, had a profound impact on Shelley and, as she puts it, *"meant she had to perk up and listen"* to what Rosemary had to say about Christianity.

Shelley wanted to know everything that was going on, and whilst I was initially quieter about my faith as an internal processor, she has since shared that she was struck by how strong my commitment to God had become, and she could see how deeply I believed all the things I shared with her about my faith. Rosemary was generally gentle in her approach, often encouraging the children in the letters she wrote to them and the conversations they had. There was one occasion, however, when that gentleness seemed to elude her, and rumour has it her explanation of hell terrified Shelley so much that it kick-started Shelley's own faith journey, which continues to this day in her outreach work in Canada, alongside her husband.

Rosemary and I both made *the most* important decisions of our lives when we accepted the offer of salvation from Jesus. Perhaps my statement in Chapter 4 that my choice of wife was the *second* most important decision of my life raised the odd eyebrow – now you know why! As juxtaposed as our journeys were, we arrived at the same destination and were baptised together on 26th November 1986, as a public declaration of the faith we now had. With the fast-paced life of a pilot, I was constantly being pushed to the limits, and as a perfectionist, the frontiers were even higher. Faith in Jesus not only saved me, but also brought an inner peace and ability to rest that I had not realised had been missing up to that point in my life. Overwhelmed by who I had discovered in the Christian faith, I was far more relaxed; I knew that I had an aim and purpose beyond me, and wanted my future to be in heaven with Jesus.

Our baptism was a significant moment in my journey, especially when Isaiah 40:31 was read out: "*But those who hope in the Lord, will renew their strength. They will soar on wings like eagles; they will run and not grow weary;*

they will walk and not be faint." A particularly poignant verse for me, it was one I would quote often to myself when faced with an issue where I needed more resolve and fortitude. For obvious reasons, as a pilot who had spent decades of his life soaring like an eagle across the skies, this verse resonated. I knew what it meant to fly high, to trust in the vast expanse of a wing span, and *effortlessly* glide through the skies, observing from above with a sense of serenity and safety, before coming in to land. To have that freedom, relying not on my abilities but on One far more competent and capable than me, was a life-defining and liberating experience which I came to embrace far more than any worldly accolade or pleasure.

10

Preparing to Land

It is no exaggeration to say my life was changed for eternity in 1981, after meeting the late Gerald Williams at the tennis dinner. More specifically, faith in God changed everything, including my flying life. As I looked upon the vast horizon before me with new eyes, I no longer just saw the night sky as a navigational tool but rather as part of the intricate design of our magnificent creator God. I quite literally had new vision. It astounds me the hours I spent traversing God's creation, navigating by the stars for six hours straight across the Pacific Ocean from Tokyo to Honolulu, deciding which stars were the best to use for my calculations, and yet only truly appreciated the flawless majesty and precision of creation when I came to know *The Creator*, the one who made it all. I don't just mean the beauty of Scotland, which I waxed lyrical about in an earlier chapter, but all of God's wonderful creation, the entire universe.

I once heard a response for an atheist's view of creation which struck a chord with me. When asked if they believed in God, the atheist's simple answer was *no*, just like my response to Gerald had been when he asked me if I would like to go to church with him! The Christian asking the atheist, responded thus:

If I gave you proof would you change your mind, for I have absolute scientific proof that God exists. Every building is proof of a builder; every painting is scientific proof of a painter. We know that because a building cannot build itself, and a painting cannot paint itself. The builder could have died fifty years ago, but we still know there was a builder at some point, as the building exists. Likewise, the artist could have died 400 years ago, but we still know there was at some point an artist as paintings cannot paint themselves. Creation is evidence of a creator; birds and trees, the sun, moon and stars, dogs and cats, men and women, land and sea – all these things are evidence of the genius of God's creative hand. Atheists believe that everything was created by nothing, but that is a scientific impossibility. To believe there is no creator is to believe that everything was created by nothing (as opposed to from nothing) and that is impossible from a scientific perspective. Nothing cannot create anything. There has to be a creator. I believe that is God.[4]

My scientific head and heart could not agree more with this sentiment.

---

4. "How to easily prove God to an atheist" by Ray Comfort, accessed 5th June 2024
https://www.youtube.com/watch?v=ETGhpcYte2I

Reflecting on my journey as I have, it is with tremendous satisfaction and fulfilment that I look back on my 804 crossings of the Atlantic at the helm of Concorde, but I do so wholly cognisant of the fact that I did not do it alone. Just as creation needed a creator, the world of Concorde needed those who made it all happen, and I was nothing without the team around me. Concorde's success was the product and pride of all who were involved in her planning, development and operation, from engineering and crewing to marketing, catering and maintenance. Over the years we developed a superb team which had, at its core, an overwhelming camaraderie and team spirit, which made it even harder to leave. But, as we all know, time waits for no one, myself included!

As the sun set on 1988 and I arrived at my fifty-fifth birthday, I myself came in to land and retired from my professional flying career. It was not, however, the ending I had imagined. Unbeknownst to me at the time, my final Concorde flight had actually occurred a few months earlier on a regular flight from New York. On that particular afternoon, as we took off from JFK, following our usual long list of take-off procedures as we always did, the meticulous process was operating with expected accuracy until, that is, we lost an engine. Thankfully, this was not as disastrous as it may sound to some. My entire life I had benefited from the muscle memory of training, allowing me to react immediately and calmly to situations in the cockpit based on the countless flying hours and training I had received, and that day was no different. Flying with the loss of an engine is part of any pilot's training and, with Concorde's remaining three Rolls Royce Olympus engines providing ample power, in accordance with standard procedure we descended to subsonic cruising altitude (circa 38,000 feet), and continued on our way.

The main impact for the passengers was that we would be flying subsonic, as supersonic flight required all four engines, so our journey would take longer. Naturally, this was to have a knock-on effect on our fuel consumption, even more so in this case as one of the intakes on the failed engine was unexpectedly causing more drag (the opposite force to propulsion) than usual. In other words, the failed engine created more aerodynamic force to resist the aeroplane's flight through the sky. When faced with an aircraft malfunction, diversion is usually an option for the captain and one that I had unhesitatingly exercised many times in my flying career. However, despite the drag, our calculations still showed acceptable fuel levels for us to return to London, rather than diverting to a closer airport, so we stayed our course and headed for Heathrow.

Though a little delayed, we landed safely in London that night. Regrettably, however, I failed to fill in the fuel log at the gate, which was requisite standard procedure. My actions, and the unique circumstances surrounding our flight, triggered a BA investigation, and even though I accepted full responsibility for the oversight, I was put on desk duty and stood down from flying; standard BA procedure being that any investigated pilot remains on the ground. With the clock ticking and the compulsory BA retirement age of fifty-five fast approaching, I was keen for the investigation to be resolved swiftly as I wanted to get back in the air for the last couple of months of my flying career. Unfortunately, despite my best endeavours, I could not expedite proceedings.

As we've journeyed together through my life story in the pages of this book, I've recounted numerous experiences and training from one conversion course to another, to upgrade me to a new aircraft or more senior position. For all the hours spent with my head in the manuals or practising in simulators or responding to the barked orders of a drill corporal, I can honestly say that this episode felt like the hardest of them all. The multitude of questions I had and the immense frustration that wished it could have happened at a different time in my career so it did not coincide with my retirement age, all made for a very trying time.

As the winter nights drew in, it became evident that the BA investigation would not be concluded before 1st January 1989 (my fifty-fifth birthday). For any pilot, the culmination of their career is the last flight, and I soon came to the deeply difficult realisation that, after thirty-six years in the air, I had captained my last voyage. I am not a man prone to effusive expressions of emotion, but to this day I still feel a sense of loss that I did not get to experience my last flight in a more celebratory manner, being greeted by family, friends and colleagues as was customary. However, that sadness is nonetheless countered by the immeasurable gratitude I feel to God that it was not the *last* flight of a different kind.

Despite the exasperation I felt at not being able to do what I loved most at the swansong of my career, the unfortunate timing and the impact on my family, I still was hugely grateful to God. Most significantly, I was, as ever, thankful that our team had once again brought Concorde and her passengers safely in to land, despite the technical malfunctions we experienced that day. I was also heartened to learn that BA's own findings subsequently showed that we had landed with fifty per cent more fuel than the minimum requirement. That said, it nonetheless proved to be one of the most painful experiences of my life, so on a more personal note, I was deeply grateful for my relationship with God at that time, realising more than ever the significant impact of that in both my heart and my head. I appreciated as never before that I knew God was with me and loved me unconditionally. I had grown to trust Him with all aspects of my life and this storm was no different. Though painful, I experienced a peace that truly surpassed understanding, knowing that I could trust Him with my future away from the captain's seat.

The hope I had from my Christian faith gave me hope for the future and life beyond the cockpit, and when faced with this difficult situation, my faith in Jesus clearly illuminated for me what I had come to realise during my discovery of Christianity: namely that everything was not all about me! My identity was not in my flying achievements; nor was it rooted in who I was when I sat in the captain's seat. My professional career did not define me, neither did my identity rest in the mistakes I had made, of which there were plenty. Rather, this whole painful and uncertain process had given me a fresh perspective of the enormity of what Jesus had done for me on the cross; my faith in Him had become an anchor, giving me a foundation on which I could stand, far away from the dizzy heights of Concorde and flying.

What was supposed to be the culmination of an eclectic and blessed career ended up being a very difficult time, not just for me but for all of my family, and the outpouring of love and support from friends and numerous colleagues at BA was a great encouragement to us all. Even when someone door-stepped her with fabricated and hurtful accusations about me, Rosemary handled it with the usual calm composure synonymous with her approach to my entire career, and I know her faith sustained her during that time. Rosemary's far more overt expressions of faith in action and ever-present calm were particularly helpful to me at this time, and I recall how she would often share her daily Bible readings, reiterating the comfort of verses from the Bible such as from the book of Isaiah 26:3, which says, *"You will keep in perfect peace those whose minds are steadfast, because they trust in you,"* and from Philippians 4:7, which promises, *"And the peace of God, which surpasses all understanding, will guard your hearts and your minds in Christ Jesus,"* and wonderfully from John's Gospel 14:27, the reassurance of *"Peace I leave with you; my peace I give you . . . Do not let your hearts be troubled and do not be afraid."*

Many a church sermon has spoken of our need to trust Jesus instead of our own good works; being stripped of pride and self-sufficiency and depending rather on the fullness of what Jesus did for us on the cross, trusting what He promised when He said, *"He who believes in me has everlasting life"* (John 6:47 NKJV). Fundamentally, the importance rests not in the circumstances, but in how we *respond* to whatever situation we find ourselves in. Categorically, I did not understand why this episode unfolded as it did, and I most certainly did not like it. That said, I was nevertheless massively reassured and heartened to discover that I actually trusted that God was with me in the midst of that storm. Just as I had registered that the chaplain really believed what he was saying all those years ago in Tiger Squadron, I was now living proof of that in my own life. This was a life-changer for me, especially for someone who, for most of their life, had relied on their own abilities and talents. The independence and ego had finally landed and surrendered to one far more competent and capable than I.

Due to my retirement as a pilot the investigation into my procedural error became redundant, and therefore lapsed. Not quite ready to put my feet up and fully retire, though my time in the captain's seat had run its course, I felt I had a few good years left in me, and accepted the offer of a consulting position with BA. I would not be flying any more, but I could still wax lyrical about the beautiful bird on the after-dinner speaking circuit – helping BA maintain important relationships with their high-end clientele. It proved a popular offering, especially for senior executives and Board members who had lost touch and sought to reconnect with the Concorde family by hearing personal updates and anecdotes of her mastery, such as I've shared in this book. Never one to shy away from sharing Concorde stories, I spent a couple of years thoroughly embracing my new-found circuit – not quite the circuit flights of my Concorde training at Filton, but enjoyable nonetheless.

It is perhaps no great surprise that my eclectic reflections of my Concorde years are balanced with a deep regret that the delta winged beauty is not in the sky today, understandable as the decisions to ground her were. I was on the tenth tee of a local golf course on 25th July 2000 when someone rushed up to me with the horrifying news of the Air France Concorde take-off tragedy and the heart-breaking loss of 113 lives. It was every pilot or crew member's worst fear, and it had happened to people the Concorde family knew directly. It was a global tragedy yet a very personal one too, and, like many, I was in shock. I knew Captain Christian Marty who was at the helm that day and can all too well imagine the responsibility he would have felt for the 100 passengers and his fellow crew members as the situation deteriorated. His feelings as the aircraft became uncontrollable and his desperation to minimise casualties on the ground, would have been at the heart of his struggle as he battled to safely return Concorde to land. I felt the pain of 113 bereaved families at the loss of their loved ones, just as I did for the family of the engaged young aviator decades earlier. Lives cut short in their prime, and memories that would never be made. It was a sickening reality to be faced with, having sat myself in the same seat on hundreds of flights, and it still hits hard in the pit of my stomach to this very day.

Alongside the understandable cries of *"Why, God, why?"* the comprehensive investigations into the tragedy found that a piece of debris left on the runway by another aircraft had punctured one of Concorde's tyres, setting off a devastating chain of events. The punctured tyre seemingly caused fragments to hit the underside of the wing, subsequently damaging a fuel tank, which in turn ignited. As a result of the tragedy, Concorde underwent extensive modifications. The work was far-reaching and the finest of technical minds gathered, determined to ensure that the precise set of catastrophic circumstances which Concorde flight AF4590 experienced could never, ever be repeated. Whilst that fateful day in July 2000 no doubt heralded Concorde's demise, the final blow was wielded by another tragic event in the aviation world.

The event was 9/11, unexpectedly the self-same day that Concorde was in the skies over the Atlantic testing those prescribed modifications. With the well-documented destruction of life, unimaginable grief, business infrastructure shattered, and the sense of airborne safety notoriously undermined, the appetite for air travel, whether recreational or business, was utterly decimated. Concorde depended for her viability on the oft-travelling business executives, who were understandably in large part grounded, and in the aftermath of this catastrophic event, when the world as we knew it changed forever, so too did the destiny of Concorde; diminished passenger demand and enhanced security concerns combining to bring to an end Concorde's own journey. Thus it was, just over two years later in October 2003, that the BA Concorde fleet was finally retired from service and the curtain came down on the Concorde era.

The events of 25th July 2000 and 9/11 meant Concorde ended her days in the most tragic of circumstances, and the enduring Concorde family will always remember the service and sacrifices of those who fought so valiantly to save the lives of others on those fateful days. Whilst of such stark contrast to the years of joy and elation she evoked in the lives of so many, I still feel pride in what Concorde achieved, not only in aviation and engineering terms but as one of the defining British icons of its era. Concorde was unlike anything I or any other pilot had ever experienced. Representing the biggest step change in aircraft performance in the history of civil aviation, she helped the world of air travel soar from a seemingly pedestrian subsonic 600mph to the supersonic 1,350mph in one giant, yet elegant, leap, and I had the privilege to be at the helm for some of her greatest milestones. Concorde was glamorous and exclusive, a technological marvel and a design of daunting beauty. I feel pride also in the hope that Concorde was the forerunner to a future age of commercially sustainable supersonic travel.

No doubt the vast wealth of technical and operational knowledge we created is being applied in the pursuit of her possible successor; a successor which will notably need to accommodate even stricter environmental considerations. Key to that will be reducing the sonic boom which for Concorde was shocking, not only in its decibel count but in the suddenness with which it was experienced on the ground; the next generation of supersonic travel will clearly need cleaner and quieter levels. That said, when it does eventually become a reality, I doubt it will do so with the benefit enjoyed by Concorde of sizeable funding from two governments, without which the beautiful bird would never have graced the skies.

I feel truly blessed to have started my flying career in an era when the relationship between the pilot, the aircraft and the skies was deeply intimate, navigating by the stars, sitting in open cockpits, flying without modern technology. Similarly, I was blessed to end my flying days in the most technologically advanced aircraft of the twentieth century. I had a good run at it, and though I would likely have enjoyed another few years, which pilots can generally do now into their sixties, retirement was overall a contented experience. Far from worrying that I could not live without flying, or wondering what I was to do with the rest of my life, I welcomed the change. Such an abundance of free time was something I had not experienced for over thirty years, and it was never dull.

I would have more time to enjoy the wonderful home life with my family, in the garden or working on house projects, and clearly recall thinking to myself, *"I've done a lot of flying and while I'll miss it, I don't regret the fact that I shan't be doing it anymore."* I was still young and had plenty of physical and mental energy as well as high hopes for life on the ground, and soon forged a new pathway. For many years I had enjoyed the best job in aviation, rubbing shoulders with the rich and famous, with ultimate responsibility for Concorde and even receiving an OBE honour from Her Majesty Queen Elizabeth II to top it all off.

Though no longer flying, Concorde still featured prominently in my new life, and bookings for speaking engagements came thick and fast. It was not just the business world who wanted to hear my stories – churches too got in on the act with Men's Breakfasts proving a popular venue for me to share my journey of faith whilst waxing lyrical about my many adventures on the flight deck. The signing of countless pictures and even latterly the writing of this book, provide proof, if it were needed, that Concorde was and always will be part of who I am. That diverse audiences continued for so many years to delight in hearing my many Concorde stories alongside those of my journey of faith exploration, always pleasantly surprised me and served as a welcome reminder of the enduring level of interest that clearly exists both in Concorde and, more importantly, in God.

11

Returning Home

Throughout most of my flying career, and for most of my life, the ever-constant support I returned home to after hours in the captain's seat, was my adored wife Rosemary. She was perfect for me, and the second most important decision of my life was to ask her to be my wife; second only to my decision to admit the relevance of the Bible and accept the salvation offered to me by Jesus. Beyond her sporting ability and musical prowess (a graduate of the Royal College of Music to name but one achievement), Rosemary was in every respect an exceptional woman. As my wife and the mother of our three children, she was my most cherished "best friend" with whom I was blessed to share fifty-eight years of marriage.

Rosemary was charmingly supportive, very proud of my career and the grounding hub of our family life. Often, I would share details of potentially serious incidents and, to my delight, there were no dramatic expressions of *"Good grief"* or *"My word, that must have been awful"*; nothing like that came from Rosemary, which suited me perfectly.

Never once do I recall hearing her ask how long I would be away this time, as I headed off for my next flight, and she always welcomed me home with open arms when I eventually returned. We were a team, a unit, each with our part to play, and we both thrived in our different roles. One time during my Concorde years, I remember her sharing her experience of a rather annoying call she'd received from a neighbour at 1am. *"I've just heard the news,"* the voice rang out, *"a plane went down and I wondered if it might have been Brian."* As it turns out, the plane was not even a Concorde, making the call even more ridiculous than it already was, but Rosemary stayed calm and did not rise to the wholly inappropriate incident.

Though she's sadly not here to correct me, I am fairly certain that Rosemary never reacted to any of the risks flying presented, except for the one time when I experienced the flat tyre on take-off, and, even then, it was just a comment. Having taken off and been informed of our puncture, we were positioning ourselves on the coast to jettison our fuel. One thing you must not do when a tyre bursts is to retract the undercarriage, given the extreme heat or flames it may be experiencing. With fuel in the wing tanks, bringing the tyres up could cause them to be ignited, and I remember very well telling the co-pilot to *"leave the gear down"* as we flew further south than usual. As it happened, Rosemary was in the garden and saw Concorde overhead that day and, sharp as a tack, noticed the unusual situation. On my return, commenting on the lowered undercarriage she had seen, she simply and calmly enquired if all was ok – nothing more! Clearly, she was used to the risks associated with flying and, greatly appreciated by me, Rosemary took it all in her stride.

When I returned home having visited hangars at midnight, fended off press packs, completed my weekly commute to New York or worked my way through a pile of paperwork at my desk, I enjoyed time with the love and support of my whole family, which often revolved around sporting activities, with tennis leading the rankings! Shelley's and Julie's tennis trophy shelves were rather extensive, filled to the brim as they were with memories of tennis tournaments both at county, national and international level. I missed many of their matches due to flying, but Julie's delight when she played Wimbledon Juniors in 1979 was shared by the entire family, and her 6-1,6-1 victory in the first round was a tremendously proud moment for me as a father. Shelley's nervous excitement on learning of her first-round opponent in the 1983 US Open echoed through the whole family. Having played her way through four qualifying rounds, she was to play none other than Chris Evert, one of the greatest of all time, who by that stage had already amassed fourteen of her eighteen Grand Slam titles.

To no-one's great surprise, Shelley did not come out on top that day against "Chrissie", as she's affectionately known, but perhaps Shelley's greatest tennis achievement rests in being one of the few players to have a winning head-to-head record against another all-time great. On retirement, Steffi Graf was the champion of twenty-two Grand Slam titles. An unheralded satellite tournament in Solihull is therefore perhaps not foremost in Steffi's career memory bank, but a win's a win and in 1983 Shelley beat Steffi 6-1,7-6 in the quarter-finals. Realistically these are probably the musings of a proud father, but given Steffi's meticulous approach to the game, part of me thinks perhaps she does remember that defeat to my daughter. Though we'll never know, I wonder if the bitter taste of that loss to Shelley helped spur her on to such tennis greatness!

As children, our kids loved flying and felt very special when "Dad the pilot" pulled some strings and surprised them with an upgrade or a trip to the flight deck. Suited and booted, as one usually was when flying in those days, I would chat with the captain as the three of them peered around the cockpit, only to hurl question after question at me when we returned to our seats. Whilst Rosemary wasn't a particular fan of flying, she did give me the honour of allowing me to fly her in Concorde on one occasion. Seated in the jump seat, like every other VIP passenger invited to join us, her awe, however, was not for the speed or technology of supersonic travel but for the beauty of planet Earth as observed from the exceptional viewpoint of the cockpit; the unique perspective Concorde provided, once again inspiring the passengers. More recently, I've had a similar joy of sharing Concorde with my ever-growing family while visiting the Brooklands Museum with various grandchildren. Sitting in the cockpit of Concorde, transporting myself back to my heyday when I was criss-crossing the skies at Mach 2, sharing stories from a different age, their infectious excitement and wide eyes reminding me that as workplaces go, mine had not been too bad.

Throughout my career, I was often asked if I flew light aircraft recreationally in my spare time or might be tempted to do so in my later retirement years. At the time, with my combined management and flying roles as they were, my spare time was scarce. Furthermore, I am not sure if my family would have been overly enthusiastic if any spare time I did have was spent in another cockpit, a sentiment I also shared. That said, I did unwittingly have one experience towards the end of my career which served only to reinforce my lack of enthusiasm for light aircraft, when a friend asked me if I would accompany him to France in a small plane. Whilst in hindsight I should have asked a few more questions as I had not previously flown the particular plane he was taking, I assumed he had and consequently agreed to his request. Confident in my abilities in small planes from the early years of my flying career, I was happy to assist by being *his* co-pilot.

The flight out was straightforward, we landed and stayed long enough for him to pick up the wine cases he was procuring. The return flight was less so. It wasn't long before we were rapidly enveloped in thick fog, and when I enquired about the equipment on board for bad weather flying, he rather anxiously disclosed that he had no flight experience for such conditions, let alone knowledge of how the plane was equipped. To add insult to growing injury, he also confessed that he was not totally au-fait with this plane as it actually belonged to a friend of his. Realising I had little option but to assume control of an unfamiliar aircraft and endeavour to bring a smooth end to what had become a horribly turbulent flight in far from ideal circumstances, I immediately radioed Air Traffic Control (ATC). Requesting coordinates for a course to steer in order to make an instrument (compass) approach, my flight prayers were in overdrive alongside my ATC conversations. Once in receipt of ATC's extremely welcome assistance, we were cleared to land and thankfully experienced a successful and much welcome touch down. What troubled me most in this particular instance was I felt misled; I had been given the impression he was familiar with the aircraft, and had made my decision accordingly.

Grateful for my safe return home, as I recounted the travails of the trip to my wife Rosemary, per norm, her no-nonsense yet supportive listening manner were the perfect unflustered response I had so appreciated over the years. Despite it all ending well, and even though I had taken the controls of a vast array of planes, from the most basic to the most sophisticated, the entire experience of that light aircraft flight back from France was as unnerving as anything I had ever experienced in my entire professional flying career. Whilst causing me a hitherto unknown level of fear in a cockpit, the flight also definitively confirmed in my mind that this would be the last time I set foot in a light aircraft. Despite the hugely unsettling personal incident, to this day I still find it gratifying to witness an ever-increasing amount of recreational flying, knowing that if recreational pilots enjoy even a fraction of the exhilaration and fulfilment that flying gave me over the thirty-six years of my career, they have a truly sensational hobby. That particular hobby, however, was just categorically not for me, and the experience had confirmed this for me in no uncertain terms as it had brought me face to face with a very stark reality of my existence.

I flew one of the most advanced aircrafts in commercial aviation history and had every confidence in Concorde, my colleagues and my own skill and training to handle any situation we encountered when surrounded by the sophisticated controls to which I was very accustomed. However, the light aircraft experience reiterated for me that when out of my own environment and reliant on somebody else's training, skills and machinery, and required to *trust them*, I felt exposed and unsafe. I didn't naturally trust others as it was, preferring as I did to rely on myself and what *I* knew. Often times I thought I could do it better, or people had not given me reason to trust them, or, worse still, had given me good reason *not* to trust them, such as this particular friend.

I was reminded again of this reality when I had the good fortune to do a few track circuits with a World Sportscar Champion. Despite the thousands of hours of flying I'd done over the years, when in the car with him I was unexpectedly nervous. Having regularly flown at speeds up to and including Mach 2 this was a revelation to some, but only served to clarify for me what I had deduced from my light aircraft experience – I didn't trust easily. I certainly trusted he was a skilled driver – he was after all in his natural environment, and a multiple champion with years of experience. But I also knew this was a sport that had suffered more than its fair share of fatalities. He himself had experienced multiple crashes, including a potentially life-threatening one when his own experience of a burst tyre caused his car to hit a wall and flip in the air before landing on its roof, his helmet top being scraped away by the track surface.

Like most of us, I had sat in cars for many decades of my life, but never one that was so close to the ground, travelling at 200mph, braking agonisingly late into every corner, over which I had no control and limited knowledge as to its capabilities. I'd accepted the invitation to barrel roll Concorde in a matter of seconds, but I knew what I was dealing with and trusted *my* training and abilities. I had come to realise that the issue for me – as I am sure is common for many people – was that I did not feel safe when I had no control or in-depth understanding of the environment which I was in. I was simply a passenger who had trusted my life to somebody else's care and protection, reliant on them for my safe return, and this did not sit comfortably with me.

I suppose I must have taken a breath at some stage, but I have no recollection of that! It was without doubt an adrenaline-charged experience, which countless others would have appreciated, but I could not have been happier when our circuits came to an end and I could return to the safety, security and familiarity of my flight deck. Having always relied on my own abilities, the light aircraft flight and circuits in the Sportscar only served to reinforce my faith and trust in *myself*, and my preference for being in control of situations; an attitude which was consistently challenged after my visit to church with Gerald Williams.

Just as Gerald had observed that day in New York when we went for breakfast, I had *everything*. Back then, when asked, as I occasionally was, what part God played in my life, my answer for many years was quite simply – *None*. For years I believed that what I had achieved had been solely through my own efforts, my own abilities, my own talent, and my many hours of hard work. I was a total egotist, entirely self-reliant, and I was ok with that. It therefore came as somewhat of a surprise when my whole mindset was proved utterly and totally wrong by the chain of events which followed that dinner with Gerald, and set me on the first step to becoming a Christian. Not only did it alter my life, but that of our entire family. Indeed, my daughter Shelley herself went on to marry Cameron, a Baptist minister, and the eldest son of the pastor who led the church we attended!

My journey of faith did not happen at anything close to Mach 2. It was pedestrian, over the course of a few years. I had a multitude of questions and I methodically sought out the answers, with the help of the Bible, Justin, Gerald, Josh's book and many other sources along the way. Though it came to me very gradually, it was nonetheless to become a strong and deeply rooted faith, my slow but steady process having created an unshakeable foundation built on irrefutable evidence and reason. I eventually got to the stage where I unequivocally believed in God. I not only believed in Him; I trusted Him and His son Jesus, who had come to earth to save us all from our sins. I acknowledged my shortcomings and sought forgiveness, and ultimately came to trust that God loved me, had sent His son Jesus to die for me, and that Jesus had given us an advocate, the Holy Spirit, who was leading me into all truth, so clearly fulfilling 1 Corinthians 2:12, *"What we have received is not the spirit of the world, but the Spirit who is from God, so that we may understand what God has freely given us."*

During my faith journey I came to understand that, as Christians, we represent God on earth and I tried to embrace that responsibility, not only to humanity but to all of God's creations. Through Rosemary's example, my own prayer life (though far from perfect) became more consistent, as I sought God's wisdom and help in various different life situations. This does not mean everything worked out as I would have wanted, but along the way I've thankfully learned to no longer worry when I don't see an obvious or immediate response. Trusting God, I feel safe in the knowledge that every prayer will be answered in His perfect timing, which, more often than not, is different from mine! Acceptance of who Jesus is and what He chose to do for me has afforded me an overwhelming security: security in the knowledge that I will be with Him for eternity; security in the knowledge that Rosemary is already with Him; and security in knowing that I will one day join her there, when I too reach my final destination.

12

Final Destination

The alpha and omega of both my flying career and faith journey were starkly different. The same could be said of my approach to life pre and post baptism. Following extensive research into the Christian faith, I came to an understanding of the relevance of the Bible, and chose to be baptised in 1986 aged fifty-two. Gratitude was a major *raison d'être* for being baptised, as I had come to view life from a vastly different vantage point; appreciating in a new way how God had not only given me skills for flying, but had also sought me and had not given up on me when I was not interested in His pursuit. On the contrary, God had given me numerous opportunities to get to know Him, first through my father and his Bible reading, then the RAF chaplain, then Gerald Williams and those I met at Millmead, and many, many others along the way. I also came to appreciate what God had given me, and that He had made me for a purpose.

As I grew in my faith journey, I saw that I should perhaps not have been so surprised by the various God-incidences which punctuated my life. I had learned from the Bible that God seeks us, such as in Revelation 3:20 where it says, *"Here I am! I stand at the door and knock. If anyone hears my voice and opens the door, I will come in and eat with that person."* God wants to be part of our lives; He knocks and wants to spend time with us. God had been pursuing me for decades. As I look back on my life, I realise so many of the "good timing" coincidences were God: God was ever present and wanted me to do life with Him. He was the source of the wisdom I sought through my father and his Bible reading; God's truth drew me to the RAF chaplain and so it went on. His pursuit of me was constant. I understand now that God gave me my talents – they were a gift from Him, rather than simply the result of my own hard work. He in His most unfathomable calculations, far beyond those of my navigator prowess, had known that Ms Rosemary Blake would be the perfect wife for me. With this new perspective, seeing the far bigger horizon of life, much like the expansive view of earth from the captain's seat on Concorde, my faith has continued to grow, deeply rooted in the truths I have come to know and love.

Appreciating in a new way how God had sought me and not given up on me, but rather given me numerous opportunities to get to know Him, gave me a hunger for more, and I was delighted to share my stories at the various speaking engagements I was invited to participate in. Rosemary's faith became inspirational to people far and wide, and she was a much-respected Bible class leader. Investing hours in study and preparation every week, we helped and encouraged each other in the growth of our faith and welcomed the opportunity to share it with others.

Rosemary was also a prayer warrior – believing fervently in the power of prayer, her lengthy morning dog walks becoming prayer marches during which she interceded for the many on her prayer list. Witnessing her wonderfully close relationship with Jesus was a particular daily delight of mine. Her own journey inspired and motivated me all the more through the joy in which she lived out her faith in sometimes challenging circumstances.

While the earlier years of my life may have been defined by flying at twice the speed of sound, the richness of my latter years have been firmly rooted in the exact opposite – my daily Bible readings and quiet prayer when I welcome the opportunity to express my gratitude for all God has given me: my family, my life and, more importantly, the promise of eternity with Him in heaven. I am delighted to know beyond any measure of doubt that heaven will be my final destination. Some may wonder how I can be so sure of my final destination and my answer is simple – because I trust what it says in John's Gospel 14:3, "And if I go and prepare a place for you, I will come back and take you to be with me that you also may be where I am." The certainty of heaven is a promise no one else has the wisdom, power or authority to grant. This verse from the little Gospel the chaplain gave me all those years ago, is still as trustworthy today as it was for all those years when I kept it close to my heart, despite not knowing the gems of peace it harboured. I don't use the word "trust" lightly, but I believe what God has said and I trust He will fulfil His promises.

Trust matters in both life and death. I trusted my team members in Tiger Squadron; I trusted Jock to help me establish the Concorde division; so too thousands of passengers trusted me as a pilot with their safety. As an aviator I know all too well how vital trust is. You have to trust your aircraft, those who designed and serviced it, those alongside you flying it, and those in the towers directing you to land it. Trust is at the heart of aviation, and so, too, my life and ultimate death with God. Whereas in situations such as during the light aircraft flight, I was far from peaceful and did not fully trust those I was with; with the Christian faith, coming to know God and Jesus, I found new peace in trusting my life to another.

As my faith grew, it dawned on me that I had met a God of love, who knew me personally and had given me so much of what I cherished in my life. He sent His son Jesus so that I, Brian Walpole, the self-confident, egotist pilot could be forgiven my many sins, top of which may well have been my arrogant faith and trust in self. The gift of salvation offered through Jesus had been offered to millions over the years and it was offered to me too. It sounds so simple now as I write these words, but as I have shared, my personal journey of faith was pedestrian, taking my time to navigate a plethora of questions about why Jesus was relevant to my life. When I did come to realise that *only* Jesus could pay the price my sins necessitated, I came to a greater understanding of my need for Him – not least that without Him I would not have access to God. This was something I could not facilitate on my own, rending all my many abilities redundant. In Jesus, and what His life and death meant, I had finally met someone who was not only worthy of trust but who could also live up to my expectations and do something that no matter how hard I trained and studied, I could never do for myself.

In faith, I met someone I could trust, someone who would never let me down. Finally, my life was safe in someone else's hands. Just as Air Traffic Control could give me a course to steer me safely home, knowing Jesus gave me the unmatched wisdom to guide my entire life. There is a reason every cockpit has a compass which always points north; if the weather deteriorates and the clouds close in and pilots feel disoriented, they can rely on the compass to guide them home. Many a time compasses have provided safe passage and saved the lives of pilots, sailors, climbers alike, providing a course to lead people to safety. Likewise, in a confusing world, the Bible has given me God's wisdom and guidance that I have relied on time and again, to lead me safely on my journey, just like the inscription from the little John's Gospel had said.

Over the years family, friends, or sometimes even strangers I have met, have told me that due to their own life circumstances or experiences, they have determined that matters of faith and religion are absolutely fine for other people, but are simply not for them – just as I determined after my terrifying experience that light aircraft travel was not for me. Clearly, I understand the sentiment and reaction to a bad experience. I certainly did not go looking for God: on the contrary, it seems He came looking for me, and I am certain that I am not the only one He pursues. God-incidences are not limited to my life only, and I have heard many stories from other people's lives which have shown all the hallmarks of God's handiwork, all further proof that all around us, God is at work. As a man of the utmost physical fitness and at the helm of one of the most sophisticated aircraft to ever take to the skies, I was no pushover when I came to faith. I did not simply trust what others told me – that was not my style. I researched, read the Bible and other books, seeking answers to whether or not God really existed. When I did eventually get to the stage where I unequivocally believed that the God of the Bible was real, it was a relief. A relief, that is, to know my life and existence was not all up to me; a relief to know someone far more capable than I was in control. I not only believed God existed, but over and over again I trusted Him to save me from my unbelief.

Trust is the cornerstone of my relationship with God because of His character, not mine. *He* is the one who is trustworthy, not me. I know I can trust Him with everything from global wars and rumours of wars, famines and earthquakes. On a personal level too, I have grown to trust Him with my family and friends and the setbacks we all face, just as I have been able to trust Him to comfort and strengthen me as I have navigated the devastating loss of my beloved wife Rosemary who totally unexpectedly died in my arms in November 2017. I remember it so well, as if it were yesterday. Rosemary had fallen over walking some months before and had damaged her shoulder, such that she required surgery. A complex procedure, she stayed in hospital after the operation, wanting to remain there until she felt well enough to return home. The joy of her homecoming was fleeting, for shortly after she returned, in the middle of the night, a cardiac arrest took her "home" to heaven.

To this day, I still feel deeply the heartache at her absence. I have no doubts that she has gone to be with Jesus, none at all, but I was and remain deeply saddened by her loss. I was grateful that she did not suffer, but her sudden death was a huge shock for those of us left behind. In dealing with my grief, I have realised that coping with death as a Christian can at times appear contradictory to those looking on. On the one hand I completely trusted God's timing of Rosemary's death, whilst on the other hand I was devastated by it. We had no warning Rosemary would be leaving us, and thus had no time to prepare, or say our goodbyes. Even so, though I do not understand the timing, I still trust God with it. Just as in a healthy relationship a child trusts their parents, even if they don't like some of the decisions the parents make – such as the insistence that it is bedtime when fun is being had – so too my trust of God was not diminished by my sorrow at Rosemary's death. I know Rosemary would have been telling me not to worry, and that she has gone to a better place.

Whilst some struggle to square the loss of a loved one with a "loving God", my lack of understanding for the timing of Rosemary's death does not need to undermine the trust I have in God, nor has it done so at any juncture. On the contrary, doing life with God, spending time reading the Bible and getting to know who He is, has provided me with a safety and security and, above all, a deeply authentic peace. Through all the heartache, the undergirding trust that God has been with me has been an unquantifiable source of comfort and strength. Being loved by God is unlike anything else I have experienced. Being able to turn to Him and ask for His help, especially during blatant misery from wounds, hurt, disappointment, illness or death, has transformed my life. No longer having to do it all myself, the love God has given me through my faith has been the most exceptional gift. Through good times and the heart-breaking life experiences, I have learned that God is utterly trustworthy, remembering the verse in Isaiah 26:3 which says, *"You will keep in perfect peace those whose minds are steadfast, because they trust in you."*

My relationship with God is the cornerstone of my life, and I pray regularly for those I love who do not themselves have one, because I know the difference that God has made in my life, and I don't want them to miss out on that for themselves. My prayer is that they will come to know who Jesus is, what He has done, and what His life means for the future of humanity, both on this earth and in our "life after death". While it saddens me that they reject God's love because I want them to experience the same peace that He has given me in the midst of the storms of life, I am nonetheless reassured, knowing God's love for them far exceeds my own and will continue long after I have left this earth.

Please do not misunderstand me. As I approach my final destination there are many questions that I cannot answer and things I still do not fully understand. Whereas before this would have bothered me as one not keen to settle without answers, now I simply embrace the fact that I do not need to know everything, conscious I can trust God with their outcome. Before I needed to understand and would poke and prod and study until I did – more often than not believing my work, life and future depended on it. But now, trusting as I do in the unwavering goodness of God, in His plan for me and His eternal design for humanity, I have peace in not understanding everything I am confronted with. God is sovereign and knows what He is doing. The final outcome of everything rests in His hands and not mine so, as Paul writes in 1 Corinthians 15:10, "*by the grace of God I am what I am*".

Whilst my log books remind me of a hugely eclectic flying career, and are valued because of that, the "log books" God holds for me are of far greater import. He knows all that I have ever done, ever thought or ever said, and one day, either near or far from now, I will face Him to account for those "life logs". Humanly speaking, that is a terrible thought – being held accountable for every aspect of my entire life in one life-defining instance. However, understanding this end that awaits me makes Jesus's sacrifice on the cross so much more fundamental to my life. My gratitude for Jesus is far beyond the limitations of human expression, grateful as I am, that through His death, my "logs" were wiped clean, as 1 John 1:7 of the Bible beautifully reassures, "*the blood of Jesus, his Son, purifies us from all sin*".

On the subject of log books of life and choices, I have previously been asked what advice I would give, particularly to young men, for whom my story might especially resonate. My answer is simple: investigating Jesus and what He did for us on the cross is *the most important thing* any of us will ever do in our life. There comes a time when the trappings and distractions of twenty-first-century life do not matter even one per cent as much as the peace, security and sense of genuine life purpose you get from trusting God and knowing His Son Jesus. Not surprisingly, I highly recommend actually reading the Bible, perhaps alongside a book such as *Evidence that Demands a Verdict* by Josh McDowell, which helped me navigate my way through my early doubts. I would not be the man that I am today without these two books and have been humbled by the writers of both! Humbled that God loved me so much that He sent His son to save me, and also humbled that Josh McDowell generously contributed the Foreword for this book.

Looking back on the decades of my life, I wish I had come to faith sooner so I could have appreciated all that God has done for me, and travelled more of my life's journey knowing Jesus, enjoying the peace that gives me, and engaging in more conversations with my Bible-reading father on the subject. When I did come to faith, I was in great physical shape. Though spiritually dead, as far as my body was concerned, I was well conditioned, thanks to the biggest worry in the life of any airline pilot – the six-monthly medical. A pre-requisite for maintaining one's licence, many a time I saw colleagues come out of their medical having been informed of a previously undetected condition, their flying career in tatters. Adamant my career would not suffer the same end, I was determined to keep my body in the best possible shape, and became fanatical about fitness and diet. Press ups every morning; squash several evenings a week; no fatty foods. I was a man on a mission, but not the most important mission. On many occasions I have however since wished that I had been as concerned about my spiritual diet and fitness as I was my physical!

As the sun gradually sets on my life, and my ninety-first year slows in pace, my closeness to God becomes ever stronger as my faith still continues to grow. My body may be approaching its end, but my appreciation of how God has blessed me throughout my long life becomes more acute by the day. In these latter days, when I've taken my dog out walking very early, sometimes at first light (as Rosemary used to do), I've seen the flow of the river, the cosmic expanse of the majestic skies in which I flew vast chunks of my life, the beautiful trees, the birds welcoming a new day, and see God in it *all*. Looking up to those ever-changing skies reminds me of God's continued supremacy, and I am above all thankful for the deeply comforting words from the Bible in Psalm 23:1-3 (ESV), *"The Lord is my shepherd; I shall not want. He makes me lie down in green pastures. He leads me beside still waters. He restores my soul. He leads me in paths of righteousness for his name's sake."*

In the pages of this book, I have had the privilege to share with you an abridged version of my life's journey and I have endeavoured to convey the difference that the Christian faith has made to my whole outlook, both in the present, the future and for the time that is "yet to come". I am grateful that God created me, and that all the God-incidences were part of His plans of hope and future for me and my family. My death, which will be one part of that perfect plan, holds no fear for me as I look forward to my *final destination* of eternity with Him. So, as we come into land, I hope you've found my story interesting but, better still, I hope it may even have prompted you to ponder some God-focused questions, so that you too may be as assured of your final destination, as I am of mine. With the hope and honour synonymous with my Concorde years, I will end our voyage thus:

"I hope you enjoyed the experience –
it's certainly one I will forever appreciate
and I wish you well on your onward journey."

About the Authors

Captain Brian Walpole OBE joined the RAF as a pilot, before entering into civil aviation with BOAC, which later became British Airways. He rose through the ranks to become BA's first Concorde division General Manager, responsible for the world's most advanced commercial aircraft. Brian was married to his late wife Rosemary for nearly six decades, and they have three children, thirteen grandchildren and an ever-growing number of great-grandchildren.

Graham Lacey has been a Christian for more than fifty years. He is married to his wife Susan, and they have two sons, Luke and James. In his working life, he traversed the globe, and frequently flew on Concorde in his role as strategic helper and trusted confidant to leaders and evangelists worldwide. He is the author of a number of books, including *Take My Life*, a book in which Dr R.T. Kendall remarked, *"I could not put this book down and I don't think you will want to either."*

Printed in Great Britain
by Amazon

61437917R00127